Sushi Cookbook for Beginners

The most comprehensive guide that teaches you step-by-step how to make excellent sushi. Everything you need to know for excellent homemade sushi!

D1518810

Welcome

Dear reader,

I am delighted to welcome you to the fantastic world of sushi. I have created this guide, packed with recipes and practical tips, to accompany you with expertise and professionalism on a journey to discover your potential in creating excellent and beautiful sushi dishes. We will be together in your kitchen, catering to every need in terms of taste, health, and the aesthetic appeal of the dishes you will create.

All the recipes in this guide have been developed to ensure excellent, practical, and easily achievable results. From now on, you can experience the exciting culinary adventure of sushi right in the comfort of your own home. Let yourself be guided, and you will be pleased with your achievements. Cooking sushi has never been so fun and accessible.

As you already know, with your purchase, you will also receive two additional recipe books as a gift—one entirely dedicated to vegetarian options and another that will help you prepare traditional Japanese appetizers, main courses, and snacks that are essential on your table. Additionally, you will receive a QR code that grants you access to an explanatory and user-friendly video tutorial.

Thank you for your trust. I will be happy to receive your feedback.

Enjoy the journey,

With love,

Asahi Dai Mori,
"Mr. Sushi" to friends.

Table of Contents

Chapter 1

Brief history of sushi

The origins

The history of sushi begins two thousand years ago when rice cultivation arrived in Japan and both sushi and the entire Japanese cuisine slowly changed over time.

It's good to know that sushi doesn't have Japanese origins and maybe you'll leap from your chair reading similar news, but it's the truth.

Symbol of the Japanese country and its culinary tradition, sushi would not have been born in Japan but in China and some sources indicate that it was even born exactly in Korea.

As we said, when the cultivation of rice arrived in Japan, a real culture began but if we really want to know where its roots are, we must first talk about narezushi or the most ancient form of sushi.

We can define narezushi as a real practice for preserving fresh fish.

This method followed a certain precise and accurate procedure in which the fish was first eviscerated, peeled, well cleaned and then filled with salt and placed in the cooked rice whose fermentation created an increase in acidity developing a perfect environment to be able to preserve it even for long periods (up to several months). This practice was therefore also useful to be able to transport it and then only after this time, was it consumed.

The fermentation of the rice meant that the fish did not go bad and when it was thought it was ready, the fermented rice was thrown away and only the fish was eaten.

For the Japanese, this ancient practice became an important food resource and an important habit for the long-lasting conservation and safe trade of fish.

It is known that the Japanese were especially lovers of eating fish with rice during the era of Muromachi (which lasted from 1336 to 1573); this dish is known as Namanare and was the most well-liked form of sushi.

Namanare was made up of raw fish rolled in rice which was previously boiled with the addition of rice vinegar and eaten still fresh and almost completely raw, before it changed its flavour.

Instead of being associated to fish conservation, this unique way of eating fish resulted in a new Japanese dish.

Later, entering the Edo period (1603-1868), a third type of sushi was introduced: haya-zushi or "fast sushi", this was assembled in such a way that both fish and rice could be eaten together "in one bite" starting to come into play even new foods such as eggs and some types of vegetables and thus became a unique and typical dish in the Japanese tradition.

In this period, the streets of Tokyo began to spread and to be popular, stalls managed by restaurateurs who sold nigirizushi, which consisted of a small brick of elongated rice covered with a slice of fish (the one that comes closest to the 'current nigiri) which required a short marinade in soy sauce and salt, to last longer.

Thus wasabi, a paste made from the root of Wasabi japonica, also known as Japanese radish, was born.

Spicy and green in color, served together with nigirisushi, it had the task of covering any unpleasant flavors and smells of the fish which, being around in the stalls, was not always kept fresh due to lack of ice.

A strange and "unhygienic" custom was that customers after consuming nigirizushi at the stall, would wipe their hands on a white curtain that covered part of the stall itself, so people would understand that the best sushi was sold there precisely because of the curtain being dirtier.

It could hardly be said to be one of the most elegant methods, but it attracted the customers.

The Japanese lived in a hurry even in the early years of the 20th century, and this type of sushi, which could be eaten with both hands and chopsticks, was perfect for them; in fact, it is a true early form of fast food. It was only after World War II that sushi really began to become as we know it today.

Getting closer to modern sushi

The breakthrough came thanks to a restaurateur, a Mr. Shirahishi, who inside his own small restaurant invented and installed kaiten-zushi, which we can literally translate as "revolving sushi."

It is obvious that we are discussing the well-known dishes carried by a belt that ran in front of the counter and made it so that customers sitting at it, could serve themselves independently.

Apparently, this ingenious idea came to him after visiting the Asahi Breweries brewery (the largest brewing company at the time) and after seeing the flow of cans within the production system from the conveyor belts, he decided to introduce a similar system within his restaurant.

Thus, another symbol of Japanese culture was born.

It was a huge success making sushi increasingly popular, even outside its national borders.

Mr. Shirahishi also invented a machine for the automatic preparation of nigiri and it was really an intelligent action to speed up and optimize its production.

He became a true pioneer and opened more than 250 eateries throughout Japan, helping to popularize and expand sushi.

Japan's economic development at the time was primarily focused on gaining access to American markets.

These were frequented by people of popular and fashionable relevance; it was really a successful trend.

The restaurateur who became most famous passed away in 2001 but his first restaurant, Genroku-Sushi, still exists and if you want to go visit it, it is located at the north exit of the Kintetsu lines at Osaka Station.

Sushi today

Japanese cuisine spreads rapidly throughout Europe and the rest of the world thanks both to increasingly active tourism that brings novelties from one country to another and to the greater attention paid to issues of food health and nutritional balance.

Sushi today has greatly benefited from refrigeration and for this reason it is treated differently, it is blast chilled and eaten raw.

There are many types of sushi that are prepared today, and it changes only according to the choice of ingredients and how they are combined with each other and the geometric designs that you decide to give them, thus creating real works of art by creating a mix between flavor and color.

In several countries a well-known system has been adopted, the "all you can eat" which literally means "everything you can eat" and there is no neighborhood that does not have one. The formula is now famous and very simple: the customer pays a fixed price and can eat whatever he can apart from leaving nothing on the plate, otherwise he will pay the leftovers "à la carte".

This idea was born with the aim of optimizing consumption and avoiding waste.

The first All You Can Eat was born in the United States to fight the consequences of the Great Depression and to entice people who were in an economically difficult situation to choose a meal out.

This was obviously a purely marketing choice that was taken by restaurateurs inspired by typical French buffets.

So, this formula, much appreciated by everyone, has become present in many restaurants.

Old stalls managed by restaurateurs

Dishes carried by a belt that ran in front of the counter and made it so that customers sitting at it, could serve themselves independently

Curiosities and tips

Among the many curiosities about sushi, the nutritional aspect is certainly in first place.

The set of various combinations of sushi has a variety of nutritional properties, but in general we can define it as a food certainly rich in omega 3, 6 and proteins thanks to raw fish, given that among the fish most used for its preparation we find salmon, prawns, tuna, octopus, and crab. in addition, rice allows you to assimilate proteins thanks to the starch it contains. The seaweed used, such as nori seaweed, is an excellent source of fiber, mineral salts, iron, vitamins C, A, B12, zinc and magnesium, and it also appears to be able to lower cholesterol and promote the elimination of fats in the blood.

The rice used to prepare sushi is sushi-meshi, a type of white rice with a short and rounded grain, a type of rice with the same nutritional properties as the others; therefore, rich in complex carbohydrates which, combined with the other ingredients rich in proteins, gives a moderate glycemic index.

The vegetables most often used are horseradish, carrots, cucumbers and they are naturally high in fiber.

In many sushi preparations we find tofu or a soy cheese, which is made up of unsaturated fats but without cholesterol and is rich in lecithin. This cheese provides good quantities of calcium, potassium, and iron. The intake of vitamins is discreet, we find in it vitamins B1, B2, PP.

Another of the curiosities that revolves around the world of sushi concerns sauces, to which we will dedicate a separate chapter. However, we can mention in the meantime that they too are rich in qualities such as mineral salts and vitamins. many have anti-inflammatory and antibacterial power, but their use must always be measured because they are often rich in sugar or salt. Having said that, it is good to know that sushi should be consumed in moderate quantities.

As tradition teaches, we must never "drown" our morsels in sauces. We should pour a very thin layer of its "flush" on our sushi. the wrong habit of dipping the rice involves a rapid absorption by it and therefore risks completely altering the flavor of our sushi and thus ingesting large doses of salt or sugar, in fact, the alternative is to lightly place the side with the fish in the sauce to also avoid that the soaked rice can fall apart.

How exactly should this goodness be eaten? One of the questions I often receive from consumers is precisely about the correct order in which we should consume it. Sushi should be eaten starting with white fish, (this is because it has a lighter and more delicate flavour), then you can proceed with more fatty fish with a stronger flavor such as mackerel, tuna, and salmon.

Finally, remember that the size of sushi is made to enjoy it in one bite, so don't cut it, even with chopsticks.

Speaking of chopsticks: traditionally sushi is eaten with the hands or with chopsticks and the latter have their own specific way to be used and if you want to respect etiquette, you cannot fail to know it.

First of all, never pierce the sushi with chopsticks because this gesture would be in bad taste as it would recall the funeral rite of the three days of the Obon of the Japanese tradition. When you are not using the chopsticks, never leave them on the table but place them on the chopstick holder, which is usually always present on the left side of the table. You must neither lick them nor use them to pass the food to another diner because this gesture also recalls a funeral custom, the rite of passage of the bones. Finally, the chopsticks will be placed horizontally with in relation to your bowl with the soy sauce when you have finished.

As far as the use of the hands is concerned, as we said it is allowed indeed you should know that in high quality restaurants and sushi bars, the sushi-man who expressly prepares the sushi for the diner often passes it to the latter from his hands and he in turn will have to eat with his hands, this ritual creates a real relationship of intimacy with the chef as well as making a beautiful tactile and profound experience with sushi. All these rules do not apply to sashimi, which must always be consumed with chopsticks.

Staying about curiosity, I would like to tell you about a particular type of sushi that is fully part of the vegetarian sushi, the kanpyo maki. This sushi is made with the fruit of a gourd plant called yugao. It has a diameter of 11 inches and is cut into strips and then dried, and it is called kanpyo. This excellent variant of sushi is prepared by boiling the fruit in soy sauce and once cooked it is wrapped in nori seaweed. We'll have a chance to talk about kanpyo maki and other varieties of vegetarian sushi in the bonus cookbook you received as a gift.

Off with one last curiosity that I have the pleasure of sharing with you.

We will learn in the next chapters how to rinse rice well and why it is right to do so, but one thing I would like to anticipate concerns the rinsing water which I advise you not to throw away, do you know why?

Rice rinse water is rich in nutrients and is considered an excellent natural fertilizer as it contains proteins, fibers and many minerals and vitamins, which are of vital importance for good nourishment and optimal growth of plants and flowers.

The starch found in wastewater will give an extra supply of nutrients just when the plant needs it most because, being a carbohydrate, the plant is able to synthesize and store it through the process of photosynthesis. Furthermore, a precious ally will be obtained for the beneficial bacteria of the soil and thus we will keep the plants strong and with a healthy bacterial population, thus favoring the creation of an environment resistant to the appearance of parasites.

What you need to know before starting

Choice of products

Now let's deal with the winning moves to obtain quality sushi, so let's start with the choice of fish.

We have two options: buy fresh fish or ready-made fish suitable for sushi. My advice is to buy fresh fish which we will then blast chill at home (we'll see how later) and therefore we need to pay attention to some details.

As a first thing it is always better to go to extremely trusted place, where hygiene and sincerity on the freshness of the products must be in first place but in case you do not have a trusted fishmonger you must always look carefully at our fish with a critical eye and for this reason the classic rules apply, such as: the eyes must be bright and shiny, the flesh firm, the color bright and not dull and a fresh scent.

In case you want to buy a whole salmon, always remember that the gills must have a bright red colour, the eyes must always be transparent and protruding and also in this case the skin must be very firm and elastic, not sticky and well attached to the bone while if you buy of the fillets, the meat must be a nice light orange or pinkish color and must be crossed by thin, clearly visible white lines.

If you buy fish that is already suitable for sushi, you will have to make sure that it has been subjected to the correct blast chilling rules, that it has undergone defrosting in compliance with all the parameters and that it has been stored separately from that destined for something else as this could contribute to contamination and in fact also the fishmonger will have to change his gloves to handle it.

When we eat sushi, we must give so much importance to the state of health of the fish as by eating it raw, man incurs an acute or chronic parasitosis caused by the larvae of the anisakis which implant themselves on the wall of the intestinal tract, of the stomach up to the colon.

Correct slaughtering of fish

Given the fact that the vast majority of people do not have a professional blast chiller at home (such as that used in restaurants) it will be necessary to use the freezer, provided that the right precautions are followed, and some tests are carried out on our domestic freezer.

First of all, we must be sure of its optimal functioning, it must not have ice or that typical sleet that is sometimes created inside it, this is an indicator that does not work in the best way. Avoid overloading with food and check that the temperature reaches at least 0.4F°, usually in traditional freezers the temperature can vary from 10F° to -13F°.

Once this is done, let's put our fresh, well cleaned and rinsed fish in tightly closed transparent film (perhaps with a few more twists) and let it rest in the freezer at a minimum of -18° for at least 96 hours.

The important thing is that this step is done with the fish immediately after purchasing it without wasting too much time.

If your freezer does not reach the temperature of 0.4°F, leave it for one more day.

Finally, avoid opening it during this time.

Once defrosted, if you don't use all the fish, it is very important not to freeze it again to avoid the development of new pathogens or bacteria, therefore, keep it in the fridge and consume it within a maximum of 2 days.

What you need

Now let's set up our worktable and see everything you need. You will need:

a large saucepan with a lid for rinsing and then cooking the rice, a large sieve for washing the rice, a large non-plastic bowl for leaving the rice to soak, a small saucepan for the mixture, a small bowl that you will use to wet your fingers with acidic water, a "wok" pan would be ideal but you can also use a pan with slightly higher sides to cook the fried food and a slotted spoon to take it out, some absorbent where you would place the fried food, indispensable then is the hangiri the typical container in bamboo or untreated wood that you will need once the rice is cooked, a white linen or cotton placemat or simple moist baking paper to cover the rice while it rests in the hangiri, some small glasses or spice rack for the seeds and other garnishes, the famous bamboo makisu mat and the transparent film for "rolling", a cutting board, a good knife with a smooth and well-sharpened blade, it is important that it is a quality knife because the success of cutting rolls and fish derives from this, a kitchen scale, a shamoji wooden spoon, (it is a spoon flat and with a rounded tip that will be used to turn the rice sideways and season it, obviously alternatively you can use a common wooden spoon as long as it is long and wide enough), finally a fan or something similar to cool the rice and make it evaporate more vinegar quickly. I also recommend comfortable and well-fitting latex gloves to avoid any form of contamination, obviously also chopsticks, the bowl for the double sauce and all the trays and containers you want to serve the sushi on the table.

Chapter 2.

The Perfect Sushi Rice

For perfect sushi, you need perfect rice

The selection of rice profoundly influences the successful outcome of our dishes. Thus, we stand ready to address the most common inquiry: which rice should one acquire for crafting sushi?

Many individuals employ the term "sushi-meshi" to denote a specific type of rice. However, this usage is erroneous, as the Japanese typically employ this term to refer to rice that has already been cooked and seasoned, often extending its application to encompass the entire meal.

Let us clarify by asserting that naturally, there exist several varieties of rice, each possessing distinct qualities that diverge in terms of grain shape and starch content. What we require, to achieve a consummate sushi experience, is KOME rice—an assortment characterized by petite, rounded, and plump grains.

KOME rice is also recognized as "glutinous rice" owing to its exceptional ability to retain compactness during the cooking process. It resists succumbing to softness, and once prepared, effortlessly adheres with a gentle press of the hands, rendering chopstick manipulation a mere trifle.

This variety has attained wide prevalence and can be procured through numerous online platforms or specialized establishments catering to Oriental cuisine. Alternatively, in the event of unavailability, one may turn to Calrose rice, originating from the United States. While its grains are of moderate proportions, they retain flavor commendably following cooking and, most importantly, exhibit an apt level of stickiness. Another viable alternative is Donghei rice, hailing from China. Possessing a sweet disposition and similar adhesive qualities, it proves suitable for the meticulous preparation of our sushi.

Above all, it is imperative to steer clear of long-grain rice varieties with scant starch content and rapid cooking times.

But now, let's see, the procedure to prepare 2lb of sushi rice:

Ingredients:

- 2.3 lb of sushi rice (short-grain Japanese rice)

- 35 fl ounces of cold water

- 7.4 fl ounces of rice vinegar

- 1.7 ounces of sugar

- 0.4 ounces of salt

- 1 small piece of kombu seaweed

Procedure:

1. Rinse the rice: Place the rice in a bowl and cover it with cold water. Stir the rice with your hands, drain it, and repeat this process 3-4 times until the water becomes clear. This helps remove excess starch from the rice.

2. Cooking the rice: Place the rinsed rice in a pot and add the cold water. Let the rice soak in the water for about 30 minutes, then cover the pot with a lid. Bring it to a boil over medium-high heat, then reduce the heat to low. Let it cook for another 10-15 minutes.

3. Preparing the seasoning mixture: While the rice is cooking, mix the rice vinegar, sugar, and salt in a small pot. Heat the mixture over medium-low heat until the sugar and salt are completely dissolved. Be careful not to let the mixture boil.

4. Cooling the rice: Once cooked, transfer the rice to a large wooden or glass bowl. Pour the seasoning mixture over the cooked rice evenly. Using a wooden spatula or paddle, gently mix the rice to distribute the seasoning evenly. Keep mixing for about 5 minutes or until the rice cools down to room temperature.

The sushi rice is now ready to be used to prepare your sushi rolls or nigiri. Make sure to use the rice within a couple of hours of preparation for the best results.

Shopping list

We are now prepared to embark on our shopping expedition, and the list I present to you below will aid in the creation of all the diverse recipes found in the cookbook.

For the rice:

- Kome rice
- Rice vinegar
- Sugar
- Salt
- Combo seaweed

For the batter:

- Panko
- 00 flour
- Sparkling water
- Bicarbonate

For the gaskets:

- White and black sesame seeds
- Leaves, flowers, and wooden sticks (for decorative purposes only)
- Pistachio, peanut, or almond cream (optional, choose one)
- Crispy fried onions (available in a pre-packaged form)

For the rolls:

- Nori seaweed
- Salmon
- Tuna
- Prawns
- Avocados
- Spreadable cheese
- Lemon

- Zucchini
- Cucumber
- Carrot
- Mayo (also spicy)
- Tobiko
- Chicken
- Beef
- Egg
- Bean sprouts
- Red cabbage
- Mozzarella cheese sticks
- Mushrooms

Cutting salmon for nigiri and sashimi

Before proceeding with the cutting process, it is advisable to clean our fillet thoroughly, as fishmongers may not always remove all the unwanted parts. Therefore, we will take it upon ourselves to eliminate both the skin and the darker portion near it. Additionally, we will remove any excess fat and the spines that are present on the surface of the fillet. To accomplish this, there is a method that I personally find very convenient. Simply place the fillet on an overturned bowl, and the intramuscular spines located at the center will be effortlessly visible and easy to extract using a pair of tweezers. Otherwise, attempting to locate them by passing a knife over the surface of the fillet could risk scratching or tearing the meat. The image below provides a visual demonstration of the process.

A small yet crucial tip: be sure to remove the spines following their natural direction.

Now that the fillet has been thoroughly cleaned, it is time to proceed with the cutting process to prepare the sushi. We will slice the fillet into slightly thicker pieces for sashimi and thinner slices for nigiri, utilizing the uppermost section of the fillet for both preparations. Remember not to discard anything, as the remaining trimmings will be used to create a delicious tartare.

Let's start with sashimi slices

Let us proceed to cut our fillet into several blocks, approximately 2.36/2.76 inches in length. Using a long, thin, and well-sharpened knife, we will remove the skin. This is a simple and swift process. The key is to hold the fillet firmly and, after making a small incision at the base between the flesh and the skin, grasp the skin with one hand and pull it while gliding the blade along, allowing it to come off easily. You may discard the skin.

Now, place the blocks on the cutting board and, positioning the knife diagonally, slice the pieces to a thickness of about 0.197 inches . Be careful not to make them too thin. Our sashimi pieces are now ready to be arranged on a beautiful platter and garnished to your liking. I personally enjoy adding colorful flower arrangements or small sprigs of parsley as decorative elements.

Let's now cut our fillet to make nigiri

After preparing our rice "balls," let us proceed as mentioned above to create our small blocks. Then, using a well-sharpened knife, tilt it at a 45-degree angle and, with a gentle yet continuous motion, make perpendicular cuts to the grain of the strips, resulting in slices approximately 0.118 inches thick. These slices should be divided into pieces that match the size of your rice balls, upon which they will be delicately placed.

Nigiri sushi offers various options, as they can be prepared with octopus, shrimp tail, and tuna, which are among the most common choices.

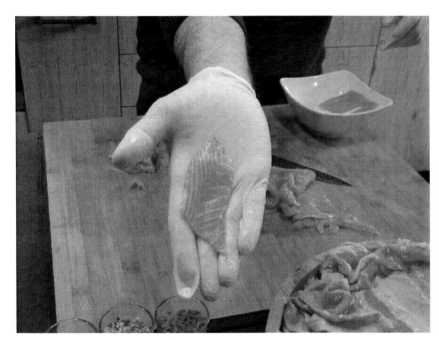

Cut for nigiri

Cut for sashimi

Sauces and spices

We certainly cannot overlook the perfect accompaniment of sauces when it comes to sushi. All the sauces we will mention can be found in stores, but if we want to prepare them at home, it is possible to do so with the right ingredients and a little patience. However, this does not apply to all sauces, as some of them, such as the famous soy sauce and others, require a lengthy and delicate process that, if not done correctly, can cause serious discomfort once consumed. Let's explore the most appreciated and commonly used sauces and see which ones we can make at home.

Soy Sauce:

Soy sauce is undoubtedly the most appreciated and widely used condiment in Japanese cuisine, especially as an accompaniment to sushi. It has a salty and intense flavor that the Japanese people refer to as "umami." Obtained through the fermentation of soybeans combined with wheat flour, salt, and water, its preparation requires a lengthy and precise process. That is why I personally discourage making it at home. Due to its high salt content, it should be consumed in moderation. Once you have purchased it, it should always be present on your table, as the sushi morsels should be lightly dipped into it to enhance their flavor.

Ponzu Sauce:

Ponzu sauce has a similar appearance to soy sauce but with a more citrusy and tangier flavor. Additionally, it can be utilized to go with meat meals, enhance salads, and enjoy with tempura and other fried dishes. This sauce is simple to make at home. Here are the ingredients you will need to make approximately 22.00 fl oz (44 tbsp):

• 6.76 fl oz mirin, 13.52 tbsp

• 3.38 fl oz soy sauce, 6.76 tbsp

• 1.01 fl oz lemon juice, 2.03 tbsp

• 1.01 fl oz orange juice, 2.03 tbsp

• 6.76 fl oz rice vinegar, 13.52 tbsp

• 3/4 tablespoons brown sugar

• A small piece of chili pepper

• A piece of Kombu seaweed

• 1 teaspoon Katsuobushi flakes

Instructions:

In a saucepan, combine rice vinegar, mirin, and the piece of kombu seaweed. Bring it to a boil and then turn off the heat.

Add a teaspoon of katsuobushi flakes, brown sugar, and chili pepper to the mixture. Stir until the sugar has melted, and let it rest for about 30 minutes.

Finally, strain the mixture and add lemon juice, orange juice, and soy sauce. Let it rest again for at least half an hour. Your sauce is ready to be enjoyed!

Teriyaki Sauce:

Teriyaki sauce is widely used and highly appreciated for its sweet and savory flavor. It is used as a condiment for sushi and sashimi, as well as for meat-based dishes, rice dishes, and vegetables. The soy sauce's saltiness combined with the sweetness of mirin and sugar gives this sauce a unique sweet and tangy aroma. If desired, you can also add grated ginger and/or garlic powder to enhance its fragrance and flavor. We can prepare homemade teriyaki sauce, let's see how.

You will need the following ingredients to make approximately 44 tbsp:

INGREDIENTS:

• 20.28 tbsp soy sauce

• 13.52 tbsp mirin

• 13.52 tbsp sake

• 2 tablespoons of sugar

PROCEDURE: Pour all the ingredients into a saucepan and mix over low heat until it reaches a boil. Keep simmering until you achieve the desired consistency. Allow it to cool, and for storage, refrigerate it.

Tsuyu Sauce:

Tsuyu sauce is made with soy sauce, katsuobushi (dried bonito flakes), and kombu seaweed. It is used to give a distinctive soy sauce and fish flavor to many traditional Japanese dishes, as well as for diluting as a broth for noodles. It pairs well with tempura. This sauce can also be easily prepared at home.

You will need the following ingredients to make approximately 44 tbsp:

- 13.42 tbsp mirin

- 27 tbsp soy sauce

- 1 strip of kombu seaweed

- 3.53 ounces katsuobushi

PROCEDURE: Pour the mirin into a skillet and bring it to a boil over medium-high heat until the alcohol odor dissipates. Add the soy sauce, kombu seaweed, and katsuobushi. After bringing the mixture to a boil, turn down the heat and let it simmer for an additional five minutes.

Turn off the heat and let it cool. Once the mixture has reached room temperature, strain it through a fine-mesh sieve.

Mirin:

Mirin is a sweet cooking's sake that, as we have seen, is widely used in the preparation of many sauces and broths. There are three main types of mirin, distinguished mainly by their alcohol content: first, we have "true" mirin, whose original name is hon mirin, with an alcohol content of around 14%. Then there is shio mirin, with a maximum alcohol content of 1.5%, and finally shin mirin, which has an alcohol content below 1% and a milder flavor. Mirin is purchased ready-made because it requires a fermentation process involving rice, water, and koji spores, which is a lengthy and delicate process.

Wasabi:

A sauce and ingredient at the same time, wasabi is a must-have at the table! Second only to soy sauce, wasabi is the most famous and appreciated Japanese condiment. It is obtained from a plant called Japanese horseradish, which grows naturally along the river valleys of Japan. Wasabi has many properties, including anti-inflammatory, antibacterial, and detoxifying properties, and it is characterized by a certain spiciness. In fact, wasabi is also known as "namida," which means "tear," because if consumed in excessive amounts, it can make your eyes tear up. So, if you're not a fan of spicy flavors, you should use it sparingly. It has an intense green color and a strong, spicy taste. Wasabi can be found in the market either in the form of a root to be grated or as a paste in a tube or jar. Mixing a small portion of wasabi with soy sauce in a small dish helps eliminate any remaining bacteria in the fish. We can make wasabi at home, and the key is to mix it until you achieve a well-blended paste.

You will need the following ingredients to make approximately 1.76 ounces of wasabi paste:

- 1 teaspoon of sesame oil

- 1 tablespoon of sugar

- 0.67 tablespoon soy sauce

- 3.38 tablespoon rice vinegar

- 1 grated wasabi root

PROCEDURE: Start by pouring the sesame oil and sugar into a small dish and mix well. Add the soy sauce and grated wasabi root. Finally, gradually add the rice vinegar while continuing to stir until you achieve a thick and creamy consistency.

Rayu:

For spicy flavor enthusiasts, we have Rayu, a delicious spicy chili oil. Made with sesame oil, chili peppers, spices, fried garlic, leek, and sesame seeds. The spices used in this oil can vary, and if you decide to make it at home, you are free to use the ones you like the most. Rayu chili oil can be used to accompany practically any dish that can be enhanced with a spicy kick, from sauces and soups to fried rice, ramen, meat dishes, or added to soy sauce for dipping sushi. It is straightforward to prepare, and you can select the spices according to your liking.

You will need the following ingredients:

- 8 tbsp sesame oil

- 2 chili peppers

- 1 piece of fresh ginger root

- 1 oz of fresh leek

- 0.53 oz of hot paprika (or the spice you prefer)

- 0.53 oz of sesame seeds

- 2-3 cloves of garlic

PROCEDURE: In a bowl, mix 1 tablespoon of sesame oil with paprika and sesame seeds, then put aside. In a frying pan, warm the remaining oil and add the chili peppers, leek, garlic, and ginger. Whisk well and cook over low heat for two to three minutes, being careful not to let it smoke. Then, turn off the heat and remove the ginger root, chili peppers, garlic, and leek. Add the mixture prepared earlier to the pan while it's still hot and mix well. Let it rest and cool down. Your chili oil is ready.

Condiment with Rice Vinegar:

Rice vinegar is particularly used as a sweet and sour condiment, obtained from the fermentation of rice vinegar, salt, sugar, and sake. It is commonly used as a base seasoning for rice and is a key ingredient in sushi. Let's look at how to prepare it at home.

You will need the following ingredients to make approximately 40 tbsp:

• 23 tbsp rice vinegar

• 16 tbsp of sugar

• salt (1 teaspoon)

• 1 tbsp sake (optional)

PROCEDURE: To prepare this condiment, you need to mix the salt, sugar, and rice vinegar in a saucepan and heat them over medium-low heat, stirring occasionally until everything dissolves without boiling. Once done, pour the mixture into a glass bottle and let it cool to room temperature.

The perfect wine

If you enjoy wine, I would say that savoring a glass during a sushi meal is essential. The choice of which wine to enjoy is undoubtedly diverse, and while traditionally sake is usually paired with sushi, nowadays a wide selection of wines is also considered.

Let's start with white wines, which particularly complement raw dishes. They can enhance the best qualities of the simple, moderately fatty ingredients with their pronounced aroma and sweetness. It is precisely because of these characteristics that opting for a slightly sparkling wine, especially as an aperitif, proves to be a fitting choice. The distinct acidity and savory notes typical of sparkling wines are perfect to accompany these qualities. The effervescence of the sparkling wine can also counterbalance the richness of fried sushi, making it suitable for fried dishes as well. If we lean more towards a still white wine, the best solution lies in aromatic wines that are fresh and have savory notes. Aromatic and semi-aromatic white wines are considered among the most versatile for pairing with sushi. This is due to their higher acidity, which can harmonize with the umami component of soy sauce, as well as the delicate and slightly sweet nature of rice and fish combined. Among the recommended white wines to consider are young and vibrant ones. Everyone has their own preferences, so there may be those who favor rosé wines. In this case, we can also give a favorable note to this pairing. A crisp and refreshing rosé, with good acidity and low alcohol content, pairs wonderfully with fish in general, including sushi.

For red wine lovers, there are some additional challenges. The tannins (natural compounds in wine that give various sensations on the palate, ranging from bitterness to sweetness, and the so-called "tannicity" varies depending on the grape variety, its maturity, different winemaking techniques, and maceration times) of red wine, along with its higher alcohol content, could potentially overpower the delicate and balanced taste of sushi. Therefore, if you still decide on a red wine, I recommend choosing one with low tannins, good acidity, and a slight hint of sweetness. This will help enhance and harmonize with the distinctive flavor of soy sauce.

Hosomaki recipes

Hosomaki with cucumber and tuna

Ingredients:

- 7 oz sashimi-grade tuna (yields 12 rolls)
- 1 piece of kombu
- 1 Japanese or Persian cucumber (yields 8 rolls)
- 1 box of natto (fermented soybean) (yields 2 rolls)
- 5 sheets of nori (dried laver seaweed)
- Sushi ginger (gari) (optional)
- 3 rice cooker cups of uncooked Japanese short-grain rice
- Soy sauce
- Wasabi (optional)
- 3 tbsp sugar
- 2.3 cups water
- 1/3 cup rice vinegar (unseasoned)
- 1 1/2 tsp kosher salt (or bottled sushi vinegar)
- 1/4 cup water
- 2 tsp rice vinegar (unseasoned)

Servings: 10 rolls

Total time: 1hr

Instructions:

1. To ensure the sushi rice and completed rolls remain moist, always cover them with a damp cloth or plastic wrap to avoid drying.

Preparing the Fillings:

2. Trim both ends of the cucumber, then halve it lengthwise and cut each half in half again, resulting in 4 strips. Remove the seeds using a knife and halve the strips lengthwise once more. This should yield 8 cucumber strips.
3. Slice the tuna into ¼-½" thick strips.
4. Take the natto out of the container and season it with soy sauce or the included seasoning. Mix well until it becomes slimy and bubbly.

Rolling the Sushi:

5. In a separate dish, mix equal parts water and rice vinegar to make vinegared finger-dipping water (Tezu). Rice will not adhere to your hands if you use water first.
6. Halve the nori sheets. Because nori sheets are not perfectly square, you should divide the rectangle in two along its longer length. To keep nori from going bad, store it in a sealed container when not in use.
7. For easier rolling, position the bamboo threads on the sushi mat so they face the side. The bamboo mat should have a half-sheet of nori on it, with one of its longer sides adjacent to the mat's back edge.
8. Make sure the glossy side of the nori is facing down and leave 3 to 4 slats showing on the side nearest to you.
9. Before touching the sushi rice, wet your hands.
10. Measure out 12 cup of sushi rice into a measuring cup. Rice will not adhere to the measuring cup if it is moistened.
11. Although it's not the traditional method, this trick ensures each roll has an equal amount of rice, resulting in uniformly sized rolls.
12. Arrange the sushi rice in the nori sheet's left centre. Distribute the rice uniformly on the nori, maintaining a 1" border at the top. Use your right hand to distribute the rice towards the right, while using your left fingers to keep the rice away from the 1" space at the top.
13. Continue spreading the rice evenly while maintaining the 1" space at the top. If the rice starts to stick to your fingers, wet them in dipping water.
14. Place the filling (tuna, cucumber, natto) in the middle of the rice. If the tuna or cucumber falls short, add additional pieces to the ends. Secure the filling with your fingers.
15. Swiftly roll the sushi over the filling, ensuring it lands right at the edge of the rice. The 1" space of nori should still be visible after rolling.
16. Gradually form and tighten the roll using your fingertips from the outside of the sushi mat without lifting the sushi mat. You can shape the sushi roll into a square or round shape. To secure the nori edge, lift the sushi mat and twist the roll gently. Apply gentle pressure to tighten the roll using your fingers.
17. To slice the sushi roll, clean your knife with a wet towel. Begin by slicing the roll in half, using a "push then pull" motion. Clean the knife once again and split each half roll into 3 pieces. Enjoy with soy sauce, wasabi, and pickled ginger.

Storing:

18. Although sushi rolls should be eaten right away, they can be preserved in the fridge for a maximum of 24 hours. To maintain their freshness, I recommend placing them in an airtight container or on a plate tightly wrapped with plastic wrap. If you cover the plate with a wide kitchen towel, you can preserve your rolls. This method ensures the rolls stay cool without causing the rice to become hard due to exposure to cold air in the refrigerator.

Salmon Hosomaki

Ingredients:

- 1½ cup water
- 1 tbsp sugar
- 4 sheets nori
- ½ lb Raw salmon
- 1⅓ cup sushi rice
- 1 tsp salt

Servings: 8 rolls

Total time: 20 min

Instructions:

1. Prepare the sushi rice by cooking and seasoning it.
2. Divide the nori sheet in half and place it on the bamboo mat, ensuring that the textured side of the nori is facing upwards.
3. Moisten your hands with a mixture of water and vinegar, commonly referred to as "Vinegar splashed water," and take a handful of rice. Distribute the rice equally all over the surface of the nori.
4. Position a thick slice of high-quality salmon, suitable for sushi, along the edge of the nori.
5. Roll the sushi tightly, applying firm pressure at each stage to ensure a compact roll.
6. Split every half of the roll into halves, then cut each quarter into 8.
7. Arrange the sushi pieces on a visually appealing plate and serve with pickled ginger (gari), wasabi paste, and a small dish of soy sauce.

Cucumber and avocado hosomaki

Ingredients:

- 1 avocado cut evensized sticks
- 5 nori seaweed sheets cut in half
- 1 piece of Kombu kelp, about 2 inch
- 4 tbsp rice vinegar
- 2 tbsp sugar
- 2 cups uncooked rice
- 1.9 cups water
- 1 small bowl of rice vinegar or water
- 1 cucumber cut evensized sticks
- 2 tsp salt

Servings: 10 rolls

Total time: 50 min

Instructions:

1. Rinse the uncooked rice thoroughly and ensure all the washing water is completely drained.
2. Add the water, a small piece of kombu kelp, and the rinsed rice to a rice cooker.
3. Follow the instructions of your rice cooker to cook the rice.
4. Make sure that you thoroughly melt the sugar and salt before mixing all the components for the sushi vinegar.
5. When the rice is done, move it to a big mixing bowl or a Hangiri wooden tub (if available) and mix it with the sushi vinegar until well combined.
6. Divide the sushi rice into equal portions of 1/2 cup (80g) each.
7. Preparing the Hosomaki Rolls
8. Cut the nori seaweed sheets in half. The standard size is usually (8.3 x 7.5). Cut the longer side in half.
9. To make the nori seaweed sheet crispier, lightly toast it by passing it over a medium flame.
10. Place 10. Position a bamboo sushi rolling mat on top of the 1/2 sheet of nori.
11. Cover the nori sheet with an even layer of 1/2 cup sushi rice, allowing about 0.6 inch of room at the top.
12. Put a cucumber stick in the rice's middle.
13. Wet the outermost section of the nori sheet with sushi vinegar or water using your fingertip.
14. Lift the sides of the bamboo rolling mat, place the cucumbers (or other filling) between your fingers, and bring one edge of the nori sheet and sushi rice across to meet the other edge.

15. Roll the sushi strongly applying some force with the bamboo sushi rolling mat.
16. Carry out the aforementioned steps with the other ingredients.
17. Slice each roll into six equal portions using a sharp knife. After each cut, clean the knife with a damp kitchen towel. Garnish the sushi rolls with sushi ginger after arranging them on a dish.

Tuna hosomaki

Ingredients:

- 4 ounces sushi-grade tuna
- 6 cups prepared sushi rice
- 4 sheets nori
- Soy sauce and wasabi, for serving

Servings: 8 rolls

Total time: 20 min

Instructions:

1. Halve the nori sheets to create pieces measuring approximately 4 x 7 1/2 inches.
2. Chop the tuna into pieces that are about half an inch thick and 7 1/2 inches long.
3. Place the bamboo sushi mat on the work surface, ensuring that the bamboo slats are positioned horizontally from left to right, allowing you to roll the mat away from yourself.
4. Place a sheet of nori above the bamboo mat (makisu), positioning one of the seaweed's long sides next to the front edge of the mat (the edge facing you).
5. Cover the nori sheet with roughly 3/4 cup of sushi rice distributed generously.
6. Position the tuna sticks horizontally on top of the rice.
7. Use light pressure as you roll up the bamboo mat to make the sushi into a cylinder. Utilizing the mat as a guide, begin rolling from one end of the mat and move to the opposite end. By pulling the mat tight and pressing down on the bamboo mat, seal the rolls securely, just like you would while rolling a cake.
8. Remove the rolled sushi from the mat.
9. Repeat the process until all the desired number of rolls is made.
10. Before slicing the sushi, moisten a knife with a damp cloth. Cut the rolled sushi into bite-sized pieces.
11. Serve the sushi immediately, accompanied by soy sauce and wasabi.

Prawn hosomaki

Ingredients:

- 12 prawn tempura
- 5g coriander leaves
- 2 tbsp sweet chilli sauce
- 2 tsp lime juice
- 300g prepared Sushi Rice
- 2 sheets Sushi Nori, cut into half

Servings: 6 rolls

Total time: 30 min

Instructions:

1. Set a bamboo sushi rolling mat on a clean surface.
2. Divide the nori sheet into two halves along the pre-marked lines, then position one half at the forefront of the bamboo mat. Make sure the nori's scratchy side is facing up. To stop the rice from adhering to your hands, wet them with water. This makes managing the rice simpler.
3. Spread a portion of cooked rice, roughly the size of a lemon, in a thin and even layer over the nori, leaving a 0,7 inches gap at the top edge to seal the roll.
4. Make an indentation in the center of the sushi rice, then place the fillings horizontally side by side.
5. Carefully and uniformly roll the nori around the fillings in the middle, ensuring that the bottom edge of the nori meets the rice on top. Utilize the mat to assist in shaping the roll, rolling away from yourself and applying firm pressure.
6. Once the roll is complete, firmly press down on the mat to slightly compress the roll and maintain its shape.
7. Using a highly sharp knife, halve the roll.
8. Divide the two halves into three equal sections, resulting in six sushi rolls.
9. To stop the rice from adhering and guarantee precise cuts, wash or wipe the knife with a wet towel after every single cut.
10. Serve alongside soy sauce, wasabi paste, or suggested sauces. Consume sushi ginger between sushi rolls to refresh the palate.

Cheese hosomaki

Ingredients:

- 1tbsp cream cheese
- 2tbsp mayonnaise
- 0.25 medium - 6" to 7" long carrots, raw
- 0.5 each avocado
- 1 sheet nori
- 1tbsp rice vinegar
- 2 tbsp Erythritol Granulated
- 0.66lb cauliflower
- 0.22lb mozzarella cheese

Servings: 8 rolls

Total time: 40 min

Instructions:

1. Dice the cauliflower into florets and place them into the food processor. Pulse until the cauliflower reaches a fine texture, resembling that of rice. You might need to work with it in two groups if your blender is tiny. Put the cauliflower rice to a pan that has been heated to a moderate temperature. The cauliflower rice should be sautéed for around 10 minutes to release the majority of its moisture and make it soft.
2. Incorporate the rice vinegar and erythritol, stirring the mixture with a spatula.
3. Place the melted cream cheese and mayonnaise in a bowl with the cauliflower rice. Using a spatula, fully combine. For about 10 minutes, cover the bowl and place it in the freezer to gently firm up. Peel the avocado and slice it into small portions as you wait. The carrot should be cut into long segments. Cut the cheese cube into small pieces. Put a bamboo mat to a spotless surface. Then, place the shiny side of the nori seaweed sheet on the bamboo mat. With a spoon, distribute the cauliflower rice onto the nori sheet, making sure to create a uniform layer. Place the cheese pieces, avocado slices, and slices of carrot across the rice, focusing on the border that is closest to you.
4. Roll up the bamboo mat as tightly as possible, applying pressure to secure the ingredients within the roll.
5. When the cheese maki is completely rolled, cut it in two using a clean, moist knife. Cut the roll into 8 equal pieces, wiping the knife blade clean between each slice. Serve alongside your preferred side dish.

Tamagoyaki hosomaki

Ingredients:

- 1 crispy cucumber
- 1 tamagoyaki (Japanese omelet)
- dash of (Japanese) soy sauce
- 2 cups cooked and vinegared sushi rice
- 3 sheets nori seaweed (dimensions 7 by 9 inch)
- 1/2 tsp wasabi or Dijon mustard
- 1 tbsp pickled ginger
- 1 ripe avocado

Servings: 8 rolls

Total time: 30 min

Instructions:

1. Peel the cucumber and divide it into two equal halves lengthwise.
2. With a spoon, remove the seeds from each half.
3. Cut each half into two quarters, and then halve each quarter again, all along the length of the cucumber. This will result in 8 long cucumber sticks.
4. Slice the pre-made tamagoyaki into strips measuring 1/5 by 1/5 inch.
5. Slice a ripe avocado in two by around the cavity with the knife. Arrange the avocado pieces on a cutting surface after removing the pit.
6. Using a knife, cut the avocado flesh into strips measuring 1/5 by 1/5 inch.
7. Place the bamboo sushi rolling mat (makisu) on the cutting board. Cover the mat with cling wrap, and then place the nori seaweed sheet, shiny side down, on top of the cling wrap. Ensure that the longer side of the seaweed sheet is closest to you.
8. Evenly spread a generous half cup of sushi rice onto the seaweed sheet, leaving approximately one inch of the far (long) end uncovered with rice. Wet your cup and fingers to handle the rice easily.
9. Arrange the avocado strips, tamagoyaki slices, and cucumber sticks in lines next to each other along the long side of the rice-covered sheet.
10. Wrap the seaweed slowly away from you, being sure to leave an inch of exposed seaweed exposed.
11. Before completing the roll, tighten it up by catching the last inch of exposed seaweed. Garnish the sushi rolls with wasabi, mustard, and pickled ginger (gari), as well as soy sauce.

Ebi roll recipes

Shrimp ebi roll

Ingredients:

- 0.5 cucumber, cut into sticks
- cooked shrimp tempura
- 1 tsp rice vinegar
- 1.76 oz plain flour
- 1 tsp cornflour
- 0.25 tsp salt
- 0.5 tsp baking powder
- 1 cup sushi rice
- 1.17 cups raw shrimp
- 2 nori sheets
- 2 tbsp pickled ginger
- 4.23 floz sparkling water

Servings: 16 rolls

Total time: 25 min

Instructions:

1. To prepare the shrimp tempura, combine the flour, cornflour, baking powder, salt, and sparkling water in a mixing bowl until you have a smooth batter with a creamy consistency.
2. In a large pan, pour vegetable oil (the amount can vary based on the pan size, but approximately 2 cups should suffice) and heat it up. Before dropping the shrimp into the heated oil, immerse each one into the batter and make sure to shake off any excess.
3. The shrimp should be fried for approximately a minute each, or until the outsides are golden and crispy. With the rest of the shrimp, repeat the frying procedure.
4. Cook the rice for the sushi roll in accordance with the directions on the package.
5. Once cooked, add the rice vinegar and allow it to cool completely.
6. To stop the rice from adhering to the bamboo mat, place it on your worktable and top it with a thin layer of plastic wrap. After that, evenly distribute half of the cooked rice over the nori sheet that has been placed on top of the plastic sheet. Invert the nori sheet in such a way that the nori is on top, and the rice is on the bottom.
7. Place half of the shrimp tempura, cucumber sticks, and ginger on the nori sheet closest to you.
8. The nori should form a tight roll when you lift the end of the bamboo mat and wrap it away from you while using your thumbs to keep the stuffing in place.

9. Trim the ends of the roll for a neat appearance, and then slice it into equal-sized mini sushi rolls.
10. Repeat the process with the remaining of the ingredients to create two larger rolls.

Avocado ebi roll

Ingredients:

- 6 slices avocado
- 9 teaspoons cream cheese
- 3 sheet Nori, dry roasted seaweed
- 9 pieces shrimp tempura prepared
- Sushi rice
- tempura batter
- oil for frying
- 1.5 cup flour

Servings: 3 rolls

Total time: 15 min

Ingredients:

1. Place the bamboo sushi rolling mat horizontally on a cutting board, ensuring that the bamboo strips are facing towards you. Top the mat with a layer of plastic wrap. Take a sheet of dried seaweed and position it on top of the mat, making sure that the shiny side is facing downwards. Over the seaweed, equally distribute an even coating of cooked rice, and vigorously press it down.
2. Flip the sushi layer over so that the seaweed is now on top. Arrange shrimp tempura, avocado, and cream cheese in a lengthwise manner at the top of the seaweed sheet, ensuring that they are placed on the seaweed and not on top of the rice. Applying strong pressure, roll the bamboo mat forward to encapsulate all of the components within the cylindrical sushi roll. The roll must be securely wrapped. Apply firm pressure to the bamboo mat with your hands, then carefully remove the rolled sushi from the mat.
3. Coat the roll with flour and then dip the entire rice roll into the tempura batter. Deep fry the roll in oil heated to 350 F° for at least 3 minutes or until the batter becomes crispy and golden brown. As a second option, you can fry the roll in a frying pan with between 1/2 and 1 cup of oil, flipping it constantly until it turns golden brown on all sides. After removing the roll from the oil, let it cool for a while. Slice the sushi roll into four to five pieces with a very sharp knife. Add spicy mayo to the pieces' tops.

To make the Spicy Mayo:

4. In a mixing bowl, incorporate mayonnaise, sriracha sauce, and sesame oil according to your liking. Stir everything together completely. Until it is time to use, keep the mixture in the fridge.

Tempura shrimp roll with veggies

Ingredients:

- 1 avocado – cut evenly and placed on top, in the center, or both of the roll
- 1/2 cucumber – sliced into long thin strips
- 2 nori sushi sheets – if using large sheets
- 2 cups cooked sushi rice – cooked and cooled
- 6 tempura shrimp
- 1/3 cup spicy mayo
- Soy sauce
- 2 ounces cream cheese

Servings: 2

Total time: 15 min

Instructions:

1. Prepare your sushi rice by cooking it and allowing it to cool.
2. Prepare your cucumber, avocado, shrimp, cream cheese, and sauces.
3. Arrange a sushi mat on the working surface and cover completely with plastic wrap or parchment paper before beginning to roll the sushi.
4. Add the rice and press it out to fit the shape and size of the nori wrap.
5. After pressing the rice with a rolling pin or using your fingers to make it homogeneous, smooth, and squeezed, cover it with a fresh piece of plastic wrap or parchment paper. Keep the bottom layer of parchment paper or plastic wrap in place so that you can add the nori.
6. Most nori wraps are huge, but since we will be maintaining the nori inside the roll, we need only use about 1/4 of the nori wraps.
7. Place the nori wrap with the rough side down and the shiny side up, being careful not to move it once it's placed. If there are any areas that do not have rice under them, insert rice under the nori as desired.
8. Put shrimp, cream cheese, cucumber, chosen sauce, and avocado if used in the center filling.
9. Vertically down the length of the wrap, arrange the fillings in the middle.
10. The rice and nori wrap sides will meet when you bring the two edges of the roll together using the plastic wrap or parchment paper that is still underneath the rice. If the sides are bigger than your filling, you can either layer them or trim off the extra rice before making the cylinder. Add rice to fill the space and create a cylinder if your filling is excessively big and the roll won't shut.
11. Lightly press the roll with your hands, then fold the plastic wrap or parchment paper around the roll. Use a sushi mat or a towel to press it together firmly but be careful not to squeeze too hard and cause the filling to come out the sides.

12. When the roll is created, pit it to a dish. If desired, add avocado on top and then add sauces.
13. To cut the roll, dip the knife into rice vinegar or water between each slice to prevent sticking. If you don't have sharp knives, a serrated knife can work well. Gently saw at each slice to create a nice sushi slice without ruining the filling.
14. Repeat the process for the second roll and enjoy!

Ebi roll with spicy sauce

Ingredients:

- 2 sheets nori (dried laver seaweed) (sliced in half crosswise)
- 2 cups sushi rice, cooked (each roll must have ½ cup sushi rice)
- 8 pieces shrimp tempura
- Spicy Mayo
- unagi (eel) sauce
- ¼ cup water
- 2 tsp rice vinegar
- 2 avocados
- ½ lemon
- 2 Tbsp tobiko (flying fish roe)- you can purchase it at any Asian grocery store
- 1 cucumber (4 oz, for four rolls)
- toasted black sesame seeds

Servings: 4 rolls

Total time: 1hr

Instructions:

1. Slice the cucumber lengthwise into four pieces. Remove the seeds and then halve each piece lengthwise to create thin strips. You should have a total of eight strips.
2. Around the pit, slice the avocado in half lengthwise, then twist the two pieces apart. Get a spoon and scoop out the pit. Alternatively, you can extract the pit using caution with your knife, ensuring not to apply excessive force to avoid injuring yourself.
3. First, hold the avocado half in your hand, preferably using a folded kitchen towel for protection.
4. Next, gently tap the back of your knife into the pit with just enough pressure for it to embed. When you twist the knife, the pit should easily come out. Continue in the same manner with the other avocado halves. Cut the avocado pieces crosswise into thin slices after removing the skin. Use your fingers to gently press down on the avocado slices in order to divide them.
5. As the avocado half is being cut, keep applying light, equal pressure with the side of the knife until it is the size of a sushi roll. If you won't be serving the sushi roll right away, I advise drizzling lemon juice over the avocado slices to stop them from turning brown.
6. For the other avocado halves, repeat these procedures. Half of the nori sheet should be set above the bamboo mat with the glossy part facing down. Top the bamboo mat with plastic wrap.

7. Moisten your hands with vinegar water (tezu) and spread half a cup of sushi rice evenly over the nori sheet.
8. Flip the nori sheet over so that the rice is on the bottom.
9. At the end of the nori sheet closest to you, place two shrimp tempura pieces, two cucumber strips, and some tobiko. Roll the nori sheet firmly over the stuffing using the bamboo mat, beginning at the bottom end, until the bottom edge is parallel to the nori sheet.
10. Lift the bamboo mat and continue rolling until the remaining nori is wrapped around the roll.
11. Compress the roll tightly and lay the bamboo mat on top. Take off the plastic wrap and bamboo mat from the sushi roll.
12. Using a knife, take the avocado portions from one half and place them on top of the roll.
13. Pieces of avocado and unagi can be alternated to coat the top and sides of the roll, if preferred.
14. Place the plastic wrap back over the roll and use the bamboo mat to tightly squeeze it, ensuring the avocado slices adhere to the roll.
15. To protect the avocado, handle it gently. Take the mat off.
16. Using the knife and plastic wrap, divide the roll into eight pieces. After each cut, clean your knife with a moist towel.
17. If the roll becomes messy during cutting, use the bamboo mat to tightly squeeze it again.
18. Place the sushi to a dish after removing the plastic wrap covering it. To create the other rolls, repeat the procedure. Add black sesame seeds, spicy mayo, and tobiko to each sushi piece as garnishes.
19. If desired, provide unagi sauce on the plate for dipping the sushi.

Spicy tuna ebi roll

Ingredients:

- ½ tsp roasted sesame oil
- 2 green onions/scallions (cut into thin rounds; set aside some for the topping)
- 1 sheet nori
- 1½ cups sushi rice (cooked and seasoned)
- 4 oz sashimi-grade tuna
- 3 tsp sriracha sauce
- 2 Tbsp toasted white sesame seeds (divided)
- Spicy mayo
- ¼ cup water
- 2 tsp rice vinegar

Servings: 2 rolls

Total time: 30 min

Instructions:

1. Prepare the sushi rice in advance following the instructions on the package.
2. Create the vinegar-water mixture for moistening your fingers (tezu) by combining ¼ cup of water and 2 tsp of rice vinegar (unseasoned) in a small bowl.
3. Slice 4 oz of high-quality tuna into small cubes measuring ¼ inch, or alternatively, finely chop the tuna.
4. In a medium bowl, incorporate the tuna, 3 tsp of sriracha sauce, ½ tsp of toasted sesame oil, and most of the sliced green onions (set aside a portion for garnishing each roll).
5. Divide your sheet of nori seaweed in half horizontally. Put one nori sheet half, shiny side down, on a bamboo sushi mat that has been coated with plastic wrap.
6. Dip your fingers in the tezu and evenly spread ¾ cup (135 g) of sushi rice onto the nori sheet. Over the rice, scatter 1 Tbsp of the 2 Tbsp of roasted white sesame seeds. The nori sheet should be turned over so that the rice side is facing the plastic wrap.
7. Line the nori sheet's border with the bamboo mat's bottom corner. Along the bottom end of the nori sheet, arrange the tuna mixture in a thin row. Holding the bamboo mat's bottom edge, roll it firmly into a cylinder form while securing the fillings with your fingertips. The bamboo mat should be gently rolled forward while being lifted at the edge.
8. Split the spicy tuna roll in half, then trim each half into three pieces with a sharp knife. After each few slices, clean the knife with a wet cloth. To keep the rice from adhering to your hands when chopping sushi rolls, dab your fingers with tezu or wrap the roll in plastic wrap.

9. Add a dollop of hot mayo and the leftover green onion slices to the top of each piece of sushi as decoration.

Spicy crab ebi roll

Ingredients:

- 0.8 pc seaweed nori sheet
- masago orange fish roe
- 1.6 pcs avocado sliced into strips
- 0.8 pc cucumber sliced into strips
- 1 cup cold water
- 2.4 tablespoon sushi rice vinegar
- 0.8 cup Japanese short grain rice
- 200 g crab sticks (kani) cut into half lengthwise
- kewpie mayonnaise
- gomashio sesame seed seasoning
- sriracha chilli sauce

Servings: 4 rolls

Total time: 50 min

Instructions:

1. Prepare the sushi rice by cooking it, then mix in the sushi seasoning. Bring it to room temperature.
2. In a bowl, combine sriracha sauce and mayonnaise. Once the crab meat is shredded, add the sriracha mayo mixture and thoroughly mix it together. Toast the nori sheet.
3. Take a sushi bamboo mat and place it on a clean, flat surface. Lay a piece of plastic wrap on top of the mat. Cut a sheet of seaweed in half and spread a thin layer of rice on one half of the seaweed. Use a spoon to gently press and flatten the rice, then sprinkle gomashio on top.
4. The seaweed side should now be facing up as you turn the rice and seaweed sheet. You can now add the spicy Kani salad from Step 2 onto the middle of the seaweed sheet. Place avocado, cucumber, and mango on top, and drizzle some mayonnaise over them.
5. Beginning at the edge, roll the bamboo mat while pressing and rolling hard with both hands until you reach the other end. Put the roll in the freezer for 15 minutes or in the fridge for at least 60 minutes. Before serving, cut the cold kani maki roll into bits and take off the plastic wrap.
6. If desired, you can put masago on a plate and roll each sushi slice onto the masago for added garnish.

Gunkan recipes

Salmon gunkan

Ingredients:

- 2 cups Sushi Rice
- 2 whole nori sheets, cut
- 7 ounces salmon roe

Servings: 10 rolls

Total time: 30 min

Instructions:

1. Take approximately one rounded tablespoon of sushi rice and shape it into a flat oval using your damp hand.
2. Make a thin border around the rice by wrapping a strip of nori around the sides, ensuring that the glossy side is facing outside. It's fine if the nori strip doesn't adhere tightly to the rice.
3. Gently place one tablespoon of salmon roe on the surface of the rice. Make this process again with the remaining portions of rice, nori, and salmon roe.

Tuna gunkan

Ingredients:

- 2 cups Sushi Rice
- 2 whole nori sheets, cut
- ½ pound sashimi-grade tuna
- 1 tablespoon soy sauce
- 2 whole nori sheets, cut
- 1 scallion, both white and green parts, minced

Servings: 12 rolls

Total time: 40 min

Instructions:

1. Dice the tuna into small chunks and finely chop it. Transfer it to a bowl, add soy sauce, and mix well. Split the tuna mixture into 12 equal parts.
2. Divide the sushi rice into 12 portions as well. Take one portion of rice in your moistened hand and shape it into a flattened oval.
3. Wrap a strip of nori around the borders of the rice, making sure the shiny side is facing outward, creating a small border around the rice. It's acceptable if the nori strip doesn't stick firmly.
4. Place one portion of the tuna mixture onto the rice and sprinkle it with chopped scallions. Make this process again with the remaining portions of rice, nori, tuna, and scallions.

Crabmeat gunkan

Ingredients:

- Freshly ground black pepper
- Juice of ½ lemon
- 1 (4¼-ounce) can lump crabmeat, drained
- Salt
  2 whole nori sheets, cut
- 1 baby cucumber, sliced diagonally
- 2 cups Sushi Rice

Servings: 10 rolls

Total time: 40 min

Instructions:

1. Combine the crabmeat, a pinch of salt, and pepper in a bowl, and squeeze in some lemon juice. If more salt and pepper are required, test the mixture and correct the amount of seasoning.
2. Take a heaping tablespoon of sushi rice and form it into an oval shape with your damp hand.
3. Take a strip of nori and wrap it around the sides of the rice, ensuring that the shiny side is facing outward. This will create a small border around the rice. It's alright if the nori strip doesn't adhere firmly.
4. Place one or two slices of cucumber on the edge of the rice and add two teaspoons of the seasoned crabmeat on top. Repeat this process with the remaining rice, nori, cucumber, and crabmeat.

Corn gunkan

Ingredients:

- 2 tablespoons soy sauce
- 2 cups Sushi Rice
- 2 tablespoons butter or margarine
- 1 cup frozen sweet corn kernels
- 2 whole nori sheets, cut

Servings: 10 rolls

Total time: 30 min

Instructions:

1. In a frying pan, warm up the butter over medium-high heat until it melts. Add the frozen corn and sauté for approximately 5 minutes, allowing the water in the corn to evaporate. Sauté for another minute after adding the soy sauce.
2. Put a heaping tablespoon of sushi rice into your damp hand, then flatten it into an oval form. Making sure the shiny side is facing outward, take a piece of nori and wrap it around the sides of the rice. This will result in a thin border enclosing the rice.
3. It's alright if the nori strip doesn't adhere firmly.
4. Place one tablespoon of the sautéed corn on top of the rice. Repeat this process with the remaining rice, nori, and corn.

Traditional gunkan

Ingredients:

- 1 tbs Ikura (salmon roe)
- 1 tbs Tobiko (Flying fish roe)
- 1 tbs salmon sashimi
- 1 tbs avocado slices
- 1 cup sushi rice
- 1⅓ tbs rice vinegar
- 1 tbs mayonnaise
- 1 tbs wasabi
- 1 tbs sugar
- ½ tbs salt
- 1 tbs corn

Servings: 8 rolls

Total time: 15 min

Instructions:

1. To start, you must clean the rice. Rinse completely it until the water runs clear. Put 1 cup rinsed rice in a pot and cover with 1.5 cups water. Utilize a rice cooker and select the cooking function. Once cooked, allow the rice to cool in the refrigerator.
2. While waiting for the rice to cool, mix salt, sugar, and vinegar in a bowl. Stir well until the mixture dissolves completely. Retrieve the rice from the fridge and evenly pour the vinegar mixture over it. Gently mix the rice, ensuring not to crush it, as it is intended for gunkan. Allow the rice to rest and cool further.
3. Measure the nori seaweed sheets, ensuring they are approximately 1.3 inches in height, and cut them accordingly. Make sure the length of the nori is sufficient to wrap the rice horizontally.
4. To prevent the nori or sushi rice from sticking, cleanse the cutting board with a damp cloth. Wet your hands with diluted vinegar and scoop out approximately 0.88 oz of rice. Form the rice into an oval and cover the sides with nori strips.
5. To seal the gunkan, use a single grain of rice as adhesive to stick the ends of the nori together securely. Using a fork or spoon, gently heap the gunkan with your chosen garnishes.

Nigiri recipes

Traditional salmon nigiri

Ingredients:

- 8 oz sashimi-grade salmon
- 2 teaspoons wasabi
- 1 cup water
- 1 tablespoons rice vinegar
- 1/2 tablespoon sugar
- 1/2 teaspoon salt
- 1 cup sushi rice

Servings: 16 pieces

Total time: 1hr

Instructions:

1. Begin by cleansing and rinsing the rice using cold water. Transfer the rice and water to the rice cooker or cook it in a regular saucepan on the stovetop, following the instructions provided.
2. After the rice has finished cooking, place it in a big bowl and let it cool somewhat. Stir an equal amount of rice vinegar, sugar, and salt into the rice while it is still hot. While the rice is still warm, stir in the combination of rice vinegar, sugar, and salt.
3. Slice the salmon diagonally, cutting against the grain, using an angle of approximately 30 to 45 degrees. I suggest slicing the salmon into pieces that are 3 inches long, 1 inch wide, and 1/4 inch thick. Adjust the angle as needed to get the desired length and thickness.
4. Take around 3 tablespoons of rice in your dominant hand and compress it firmly into an oval shape. Ensure that the bottom is flat while maintaining a rounded top. To avoid clinging, you can dip your hand in tezu water.
5. Position the salmon slice on the base of your fingers, then take a small portion of wasabi, approximately the size of a pea, and spread it in the center of the fish.
6. Place the formed sushi rice on top of the salmon and use your fingers to fold and cover both the fish and rice together. Apply gentle pressure with the index finger of your other hand to compact the rice.
7. Flip the fish and rice combination, allowing the salmon slice to rest on top of the rice. Serve the sushi with optional accompaniments such as additional wasabi or soy sauce.

Tuna nigiri

Ingredients:

- ½ pound sashimi-grade tuna, sliced
- 2 tablespoons pickled sushi ginger
- 2 cups Sushi Rice
- Wasabi
- Soy sauce

Servings: 10 pieces

Total time: 20 min

Instructions:

1. Take a generous tablespoon of sushi rice using your damp hand and shape it into a compact oval form resembling a football.
2. Apply a small amount of wasabi in the center of the rice, then layer a piece of tuna over it, gently pressing the fish onto the rice. Carefully transfer the assembled sushi to a serving plate.
3. Repeat this process with the remaining rice, wasabi, and tuna.
4. Position the ginger on one corner of the plate or provide a small bowl alongside it.
5. Additionally, serve each person with an individual shallow dish of soy sauce.

Beef nigiri

Ingredients:

- ¼ teaspoon wasabi
- 1 tablespoon soy sauce
- 6 ounces sirloin steak, chuck steak, or rib eye steak, sliced into 1-by-2-inch pieces, ¼ to ½ inch thick
- 2 scallions, white and green parts, trimmed
- 2 cups Sushi Rice

Servings: 12 pieces

Total time: 20 min

Instructions:

1. Preheat a dry skillet over medium heat for a few minutes, then proceed to sear the beef on one side for approximately 3 to 4 minutes.
2. Meanwhile, combine the wasabi and soy sauce in a mixing bowl.
3. Flip the beef over, pour the sauce over it, and continue cooking for an additional 3 to 4 minutes until the beef achieves a brown color. Set it aside.
4. Using your damp hand, scoop a heaping tablespoon of sushi rice and shape it into a flattened oval form, resembling a football. Repeat this step with the remaining rice.
5. Allow the beef to cool down sufficiently before placing a piece on top of each rice mound. Transfer the assembled sushi to a serving dish and garnish it with scallions.

Chicken nigiri

Ingredients:

- ½ tablespoon soy sauce
- ½ tablespoon mirin
- 1 tablespoon vegetable oil
- 2 medium boneless, skinless chicken thighs
- 2 cups Sushi Rice
- 10 (½-by-4-inch) nori strips
- ½ tablespoon cooking sake, plus 1 teaspoon
- ½ teaspoon sugar

Servings: 12 pieces

Total time: 25 min

Instructions:

1. Warm the vegetable oil in a pan over medium heat until it glistens.
2. Put the chicken and cook for 4 minutes. Flip the chicken over, pour in ½ tablespoon of cooking sake, cover the pan, and lower the heat to low. Allow the chicken to steam for 3 minutes.
3. Next, add the remaining 1 teaspoon of cooking sake, mirin, sugar, and sugar to the skillet. Increase the heat to medium and let it simmer for 6 minutes.
4. Occasionally turn the chicken and use a spoon to baste it with the sauce, ensuring the chicken is coated well. Cook until almost all of the sauce has been reduced.
5. Allow the chicken to cool, then slice it into pieces that are approximately ½ inch thick.
6. Using your moistened hand, scoop a generous tablespoon of sushi rice and shape it into a flat oval.
7. Place a piece of chicken on top of the rice. Secure the chicken by wrapping a strip of nori horizontally around it, ensuring the seam is on the bottom.
8. Arrange the sushi with the seam side down on a serving plate.
9. Make this process again with the remaining rice, chicken, and nori.

Sashimi recipes

Salmon sashimi

Ingredients:

- 1 tablespoon citrus ponzu sauce
- ¼ teaspoon pressed or minced garlic
- 5-6 oz salmon
- ½ teaspoon wasabi
- 1 tablespoon pickled ginger
- 4 tablespoon soy sauce
- ¼ teaspoon wasabi
- ¼ teaspoon fresh lemon juice
- 5-6 slices lemon

Servings: 4

Total time: 5 min

Instructions:

1. Slice the salmon into thin, rectangular pieces, resembling sashimi-style cuts. Aim for slices that are about ¼ inch thick or adjust according to your preference.
2. Combine soy sauce and tangy yuzu ponzu sauce to create a delectable dipping sauce. You can also use them separately as individual dipping sauces. For a variation, consider making a garlic-infused ponzu sauce by adding a small amount of crushed or finely chopped garlic to your ponzu mixture.
3. Prepare a tasty dipping sauce by mixing soy sauce, wasabi, and lemon juice. While lemon juice is not traditionally used, it adds a delightful tangy flavor to the sauce.
4. As accompaniments, serve pickled ginger and wasabi on the side. Remember to enjoy the dish immediately and avoid storing it for later consumption.

Tuna sashimi

Ingredients:

- wasabi, to taste
- 1"-piece fresh ginger
- 0.5 lb Sushi-grade Fresh Tuna
- soy sauce, to taste

Servings: 8 pieces

Total time: 10 min

Instructions:

1. To facilitate the slicing process, place the tuna in the freezer for a duration of 10 minutes. This brief chilling period will make it more manageable to slice.
2. Proceed to slice the tuna into thin pieces, cutting against the grain. Aim for slices that measure approximately 1/8" to 1/4" in thickness.
3. Arrange the sliced tuna on a spacious serving platter, ensuring that they slightly overlap for an appealing presentation.
4. Enhance the dish by adorning it with small portions of wasabi and ginger as decorative elements.
5. It is crucial to serve the tuna immediately to preserve its freshness. Accompany the dish with soy sauce, providing a savory dipping option for a delightful culinary experience.

Scallop sashimi

Ingredients:

- 4 sashimi-grade scallops, halved horizontally
- 1 teaspoon natural sea salt
- 1 green leaf lettuce leaf, torn into 4 pieces
- Wasabi
- 4 tablespoons salmon roe

Servings: 4 pieces

Total time: 10 min

Instructions:

1. Cover a serving plate with lettuce leaves, place two scallop slices on each lettuce leaf, and position the salt in the corner of the plate.
2. Take a deep, small plate and add one tablespoon of salmon roe, then sprinkle a small amount of wasabi on top. Repeat this process for three additional plates using the remaining salmon roe and wasabi.

Sashimi mix

Ingredients:

- 1 teaspoon wasabi
- ½ pound sashimi-grade tuna, sliced
- ¼ small daikon radish, shredded
- 1 green leaf lettuce leaf, torn
- Soy sauce
- ½ pound seared bonito, sliced in ⅓-inch-wide pieces
- ½ pound sashimi-grade salmon, sliced

Servings: 8 pieces

Total time: 10 min

Instructions:

1. Cover a serving plate with thin slices of daikon radish, arrange the lettuce leaves on top of the daikon, and create a small pile of wasabi in one corner of the plate.
2. Next, place the slices of tuna, salmon, and bonito fish on the bed of lettuce.
3. Finally, serve the dish with individual small dishes of soy sauce for each person.

Tartar recipes

Classic salmon tartar

Ingredients:

- 1 1/2 teaspoons grapeseed or vegetable oil
- 1/4 cup finely diced, seeded cucumber
- 1 tablespoon fresh lime juice
- 1 8-ounce boneless salmon fillet, skinless
- 1 1/2 teaspoons minced shallot
- 1/4 teaspoon (scant) lime zest
- 1/2 teaspoon Asian sesame oil
- Kosher salt

Servings: 4

Total time: 40 min

Instructions:

1. Put the salmon onto a plate and put it in the freezer for at least 20 minutes until it becomes well chilled.
2. With a sharp knife, thinly slice the salmon lengthwise into sheets that are about 1/8 inch wide. Take each sheet and cut it into strips that are 1/8 inch long. Then, crosswise, cut the strips into cubes that are also 1/8 inch in size.
3. Take a medium-sized bowl and place the salmon cubes in it. Add the cucumber and other specified ingredients and mix everything together gently. Ensure that the tartare is well combined. Season the tartare with salt and pepper according to your taste.
4. Finally, transfer the prepared tartare to a separate serving bowl.

Salmon tartar with avocado

Ingredients:

- 2 eschalots, finely chopped
- 1 large avocado, finely chopped
- 1/2 tsp grated fresh wasabi
- 0.66lb sashimi-grade salmon, finely chopped
- 4 wasabi leaves
- 1 cup micro herbs
- 2 tbs olive oil
- 2 tbs finely chopped chives
- 1 cup tempura flour
- 1 cup vegetable oil, to fry
- 2 tsp sesame oil
- 2 tbs mirin
- 1/4 cup light soy sauce

Servings: 4

Total time: 30 min

Instructions:

1. In a bowl, mix together the salmon, olive oil, chopped herbs, and finely chopped shallots. Drizzle the mixture with salt and pepper, then refrigerate it for 30 minutes to chill.
2. In another bowl, mash the avocado and grated wasabi together until it becomes a smooth consistency. Season the mashed avocado and set it aside.
3. To prepare the tempura batter, whisk the flour with 3/4 cup of cold water until you have a loose batter. Set the batter aside.
4. For the dressing, combine all the ingredients in a separate bowl and set it aside.
5. Place ring molds measuring approximately 2.3 inches in diameter onto individual plates. Fill each mold halfway with the salmon tartare mixture. After, distribute the mashed avocado over the top to fill the rest of the mold. Carefully remove the ring molds to reveal the layered presentation.
6. In another pan, warm up the vegetable oil until it reaches a temperature of 374 F. You can test if the oil is warm enough by dipping a cube of bread - it should turn golden in about 30 seconds. Dip the wasabi leaves into the tempura batter and fry them until they become crisp. Gently remove the fried leaves with a spoon and set them on a paper cloth to absorb extra oil.
7. To serve, arrange micro herbs on top of the avocado layer, drizzle the dressing over the dish, and garnish with the fried wasabi leaves.

Tuna tartar

Ingredients:

- 1 Stalk Green Onion
- 4 Shiso Leaves
- 2 tsp Soy Sauce
- 2 Inch Lotus Roots or rice cracker
- 1/4 Cup Neutral Cooking Oil
- 1 tsp Sesame Oil
- 1/8 tsp Toasted Sesame Seed
- 1/2 lb Sushi/Sashimi Grade Yellowfin Tuna
- 1/8 tsp Salt

Servings: 10 bites

Total time: 7 min

Instructions:

1. Peel and thinly cut slices of lotus roots as required (approximately 8-10 slices). In a non-stick frying pan, add a neutral cooking oil (enough to cover half an inch from the pan's bottom) and heat it over medium-high heat.
2. When the oil is warmed, put the sliced lotus roots, and cook them for about 30-45 seconds per side, or until they turn brown.
3. Then, transfer the cooked lotus roots to a cooling rack. If you are using rice crackers, you can skip these steps.
4. Finely dice the yellowfin tuna. Chop the green onions and shiso leaves as demonstrated in the instructions. Stir and incorporate the chopped yellowfin tuna, finely cut green onions, minced shiso leaves, soy sauce, salt, and sesame oil in a little bowl.
5. Take one tablespoon of the tuna tartare mixture and place it on top of a lotus root chip.
6. Finish it off by sprinkling toasted sesame seeds on top.

Futomaki recipes

Futomaki with veggies

Ingredients:

- 2/3 cup dashi stock
- 3 tbsp soy sauce
- 1-ounce dried kanpyo (calabash gourd)
- Water, for soaking
- 4 tbps granulated sugar
- 1 tsp mirin
- 1 tsp Canola oil
- 2 large eggs
- 6 cups cooked sushi rice
- 1 small cucumber, quartered lengthwise
- 4 sheets nori

Servings: 4

Total time: 110 min

Instructions:

1. In a small dish, clean and rinse kanpyo (dried calabash gourd). Submerge it in fresh water for approximately 1 hour until it becomes soft and flexible. Squeeze out any excess water from the kanpyo.
2. Cut the softened kanpyo into pieces that are around 8 inches in length.
3. In a medium-sized pot, combine dashi broth, soy sauce, 2 tablespoons of sugar, and mirin. Bring this combination to a boil over medium-high heat.
4. Add the kanpyo and let it simmer over low flame until most of the liquid has evaporated. Allow it to cool.
5. For the tamagoyaki, beat eggs and 2 tablespoons of sugar together in a small bowl.
6. Warm canola oil in a frying pan, ensuring that the pan is well coated with oil. Pour the egg mixture into the pan, creating a thin layer.
7. Carefully roll or fold the egg omelet to create a thick roll.
8. Remove it from the pan and let it cool before cutting it into long sticks.
9. A covering of plastic wrap should be placed over the bamboo mat to make cleaning easier. On the bamboo mat, spread an adequate amount of dried, roasted seaweed (nori) on top of the plastic wrap.
10. Over the nori sheet, equally spread one-fourth of the sushi rice. On top of the rice in the middle, place the kanpyo, omelet, and cucumber sticks horizontally. Using pressure, tightly roll the bamboo mat to form the sushi into a cylindrical shape.

Remove the bamboo mat from the sushi roll by pressing it firmly. Make three more futomaki rolls by repeating this procedure.

11. Before slicing the futomaki, wipe the knife with a damp cloth.

12. Roll the sushi and slice it into small portions.

Salmon futomaki

Ingredients:

- 1 bunch of chives
- 2 sheets of nori
- 2.8-3.5 ounces of fresh, sashimi-quality salmon fillet, approximately 0.4 inches thick, skinned and boned
- 1 avocado
- approximately 2 cups (about 10.6 ounces) of cooked sushi rice
- 5.3ounces of white crabmeat

Servings: 8/10 pieces

Total time: 30 min

Instructions:

1. Slice the salmon lengthwise into strips that are approximately 0.4 inches wide. From an 2.8-3.5-ounce slice of salmon, you should be able to obtain 2 strips that are about 7.9 inches long.
2. Slice the avocado in half lengthwise around the pit. Twist and separate the two halves.
3. Holding the half with the pit, tap the pit firmly and carefully with the sharp tip of a knife blade, then twist to easily remove the pit.
4. Peel the skin neatly and slice the avocado lengthwise into crescent-shaped pieces that are approximately 0.2 inches wide. Wash the chives and leave them as whole strands.
5. The nori seaweed sheets will have some thin lines visible.
6. Make sure the lines on the sheet are horizontally aligned throughout the mat by placing the entire sheet with the shiny side down at the bottom of the sushi mat.
7. Moisten your fingers in a bowl of water and remove any excess moisture. Damp fingers are helpful when handling sticky sushi rice.
8. Locate the second line from the top of the nori sheet, approximately 1.2-1.6 inches down.
9. Leave the top 1.2-1.6 inches of the sheet clear, and evenly and gently spread a handful of rice (roughly 5.6 ounces) over the sheet using your fingertips.
10. Avoid using excessive rice and do not press it onto the sheet. Rice should be spread out in a very thin layer.
11. With the length of the nori sheet, place the rice in the middle, followed by half of the salmon, chives, crabmeat, and avocado. Wasabi can be added to the rice before the other ingredients, if preferred.
12. Begin rolling from the bottom edge of the nori sheet to the top edge of the rice while holding the contents in place with your index fingers. Roll three or four times,

opening the mat after each roll to ensuring there are no gaps between the fillings and the nori.

13. Repeat the process with the rest of the nori sheet and filling ingredients, then divide each roll into 8-10 pieces.

Futomaki with tuna, salmon and avocado

Ingredients:

- 1 avocado, ripe but firm
- 2 sheets of nori
- 2.8-3.5 ounces fresh, sashimi-quality salmon fillet, 0.4 inches thick, skinned and deboned (ask your fishmonger to do this for you)
- 2.8-3.5 ounces fresh, sashimi-quality tuna steak, 0.4 inches thick (ask your fishmonger to prepare it for you)
- 11.3ounces of sushi rice
- 2 tablespoons of tobiko (flying-fish roe)

Servings: 8/10 pieces

Total time: 35 min

Instructions:

1. Slice the salmon lengthwise into strips that are 0.4 inches wide. You should be able to obtain 2 strips measuring 7.9 inches in length from an 2.8-3.5-ounce slice of salmon Repeat the process with the tuna steak.
2. Halve the avocado lengthwise around the pit.
3. Twist and separate the two halves. With the half containing the pit, gently tap the pit with the sharp end of a knife blade and twist it out - the pit should come out easily.
4. Peel the avocado skin neatly and cut the flesh lengthwise into crescent-shaped pieces that are 0.4 inches wide.
5. Place a complete nori sheet at the bottom of the sushi mat, aligning the lines of the sheet horizontally. The nori won't be exposed in the finished roll, so it isn't important if the shiny part is facing up or down.
6. Shake off any extra water after dipping the fingertips in the bowl of water.
7. Moistened fingers are helpful when handling sticky sushi rice. Locate the second line from the bottom of the nori sheet, around 1.2-1.6 inches up.
8. Leaving the bottom 1.2-1.6 inches clear, evenly, and gently spread a handful (approximately 5.6 ounces) of rice over the nori sheet using your fingertips. Avoid using too much rice and refrain from pressing it onto the sheet. The layer of rice should be very thin.
9. Sprinkle 1 tablespoon of tobiko or masago over the rice, which will end up on the outside of the roll. Turn the nori sheet over on the mat while holding the left side in both hands so that the nori is facing up.
10. Arrange half of the salmon, half of the avocado strips, and half of the tuna in a single row at the base of the nori on the rice-free section.

11. Arrange them all on the clear part of the nori just below the rice. If desired, you can add some wasabi to the nori before adding the fillings.
12. To roll the sushi, follow the rolling instructions provided below.
13. Repeat the process with the remaining nori sheet and fillings, then proceed to cut the rolls as described.

Rolling the sushi:

14. Starting from the bottom border of the nori sheet and moving up to the top edge of the rice, roll the sushi while holding the fillings in place with your index fingers. Roll it 3 or 4 times, making sure to open the mat each time and tightly roll it to eliminate any gaps between the fillings and the nori.

Cutting the sushi:

15. Take the sushi roll off the mat and set it on a dry, spotless working table. Slice each roll into 8–10 bits utilizing a sharp knife that has been moistened. Ensure your cuts are smooth and quick. I recommend wiping the knife clean after each cut.

Traditional tuna futomaki

Ingredients:

- 5.3oz cooked sushi rice
- to taste wasabi
- 1 sheet of nori seaweed
- 0.5 oz surimi
- 0.4 oz fish roe or flying fish roe
- 0.7 oz cucumbers or thinly sliced carrot sticks
- 1.4 oz tuna
- 0.5 oz ripe avocado
- to taste wasabi
- to taste soy sauce
- to taste pickled ginger

Servings: 12 pieces

Total time: 30 min

Instructions:

1. To prepare the futomaki, place a whole sheet of nori seaweed on a bamboo mat (if desired, you may cover it with plastic wrap), with the smooth and shiny side facing down. Wet your hands in a bowl of water, preferably mixed with a few tablespoons of rice vinegar, and take about 3.5 oz of sushi rice.
2. Wetting your hands is necessary to prevent the sticky rice from sticking to your hands. Distribute the rice equally over the surface of the nori (you can use a wooden spatula to help), leaving 0,78 inches of nori free at the top edge.
3. The rice should not be too thick. If desired, you can take a small amount of wasabi and spread it in the center of the rice, but not too much as wasabi is spicy.
4. Take approximately a spoonful of fish roe and place it in the center of the rice, then arrange the sticks of various ingredients in a way that you prefer.
5. You can also increase the amount of wasabi by sprinkling it on the surface of the fish.
6. Fill the futomaki with salmon roe, a halved surimi, sticks of fresh tuna, cucumber strips, avocado strips (which should be soft and ripe), or blanched carrot strips to make them more tender.
7. Remember that the sticks should have a thickness of about 0,39 inches and should be placed in the center, trimming any excess, or adding additional pieces to cover the entire length of the roll.
8. Take the bottom edge of the bamboo mat and wrap everything up like a burrito by squeezing the centre component inside with your fingertips.

9. Maintain gentle pressure on the roll to keep it compact until you see the uncovered strip of nori; then, slightly advance the roll so that the uncovered strip of nori seals it all together – the moisture from the rice will act as adhesive.

10. At this point, shape the roll by pressing evenly with your hands along its length.

11. Push any protruding rice grains back inside. All that's left is to cut the futomaki: place it on a cutting board and wet the blade of the knife with the rice vinegar-water mixture.

12. To make 12 pieces of futomaki, divide it in half, lay the two halves side by side, and then chop them into six equal-sized pieces.

Fried futomaki

Ingredients:

- 5.3oz Sushi Rice
- 0.7 oz Avocado
- 0.9 oz Cream Cheese
- 1.4 oz Salmon
- 1 sheet Nori Seaweed
- Oil of Peanut (as needed)

For the batter:

- 10.1 fl oz Sparkling Water
- 3.5 oz All-Purpose Flour
- 3.5oz Rice Flour
- Ice (as needed)

Servings: 10 pieces

Total time: 30 min

Instructions:

1. After preparing the sushi rice, cut both the salmon and avocado into 0.39 inches sticks after peeling them.
2. Spread a sheet of seaweed and fill it with a layer of rice, evenly distributing it with your hands and leaving about 0,78 inches of seaweed free on the long side. Then place the salmon and avocado sticks, as well as the spreadable cream cheese, in the center. Roll it tightly.
3. Prepare the batter with all the necessary ingredients, keeping them very cold. Mix the flours in a bowl, then place them in a larger container filled with ice. Add the sparkling water, stirring quickly with a whisk until you obtain a lumpy mixture.
4. Heat abundant vegetable oil in a wok (350°F) and fry the tempura batter in it. When the oil has reached the right temperature, dip the roll into the batter and fry it until evenly golden.
5. Drain it on kitchen paper towels and, using a knife moistened with water, divide the roll in half. Place the two pieces side by side and slice them into 5 equal parts. Serve accompanied by soy sauce, wasabi, and pickled ginger.

Shrimp futomaki

Ingredients:

- 1 small Japanese cucumber, sliced into strips
- 2 teaspoons refined salt
- 3 sheets nori
- 3 cups sushi rice shari
- 4 ¼ cups sushi vinegar
- Wasabi
- 4 cups cooked rice, seasoned with sushi vinegar
- 15-20 large shrimp, cooked
- ⅓ cup finely grated carrot
- Soy sauce
- 3 pieces imitation crab sticks, halved lengthwise
- 1 avocado, pitted, peeled, cut into strips
- 2 leaves romaine lettuce, minced

Sushi vinegar:

- 3 ½ cups water
- ½ cup rice vinegar
- 2 tablespoons white sugar
- Sushi ginger

Vinegar water for dipping hands (Tezu):

- ¼ cup water
- 2 teaspoons rice vinegar

Servings: 8 pieces

Total time: 30 min

Instructions:

1. Combine the mixture for sushi seasoning in a skillet and gently warm it up on the stovetop over medium heat. Mix until everything is melted. (As a second option, you might microwave the vinegar mixture to reheat it). Put the rice in a fine strainer and thoroughly rinse with cold water from the faucet.
2. Ensure thorough drainage. Transfer the rice to a sturdy pot and add the water, ensuring a level surface. Bring the saucepan to a boil, then reduce the heat to low and cover it.
3. If the boiling liquid starts to overflow, briefly remove the lid to let it settle and promptly replace the lid.

4. Let the rice soak up all the water. Watch out for burning. If you smell anything burning, turn off the heat right away and allow the residual heat to finish the cooking. When all the water has been absorbed, the rice should be done.
5. Split all the ingredients into 4 equal quantities so there will be 4 rolls.
6. When assembling the filling, arrange a row of 5-6 shrimp about 2 inches from the edge nearest to you. Follow with a row of crab sticks and a row of shredded lettuce. On top of the shrimp, place avocado slices and shredded lettuce, arranging them like stacked logs.
7. Cut each roll into 8 pieces. Enjoy with soy sauce, wasabi, and pickled ginger.

Surimi futomaki

Ingredients:

Sauce:

- 1 tsp lemon juice
- 1 tbsp kewpie Japanese mayonnaise

Fillings:

- 4 kanikama surimi crab sticks
- 4 inches cucumber
- ¼ avocado

Wrapping:

- 2 sheets nori
- 9 ounces short grain sushi rice pre-made with seasoning

For serving:

- 2 tbsp soy sauce in a sauce

Servings: 4 rolls

Total time: 20 min

Instructions:

1. Prepare the kanikama by patting it dry using a kitchen towel. Proceed to halve them lengthwise, creating two thin strips.
2. Slice the cucumber into thin strips and peel the avocado. Cut it into strips, slightly larger in size. To prevent browning, drizzle a bit of lemon juice over the avocado strips.
3. Grab the bamboo sushi mat and top it with plastic wrap. Using a spoon, place half of the rice on top of the mat (as you will be making two rolls). Distribute the rice uniformly over the nori sheet using wet fingertips, creating a tiny gap at the bottom and top edges for closing the rolls.
4. Arrange a thin layer of mayonnaise over the rice to enhance its stickiness. Arrange the kanikama strips on top, followed by avocado and cucumber slices (remember, you're using only half the ingredients for one roll as you will be making two).
5. Carefully roll the maki using the bamboo mat, ensuring precision and tightness.
6. Once rolled, the futomaki is ready to be served. Slice it into eight equal round pieces and proceed to make the second roll.
7. Present the rolls on a plate, accompanied by a small dish of soy sauce on the side.

Futomaki like a chef

Ingredients:

- 2 tablespoons vegetable oil
- 1 tablespoon sugar
- 4 eggs
- 2 tablespoons rice wine
- Soy sauce (to taste)
- 1 pinch salt
- 4 surimi
- 4 tablespoons white sesame seeds
- 4 tablespoons vinegar
- 4 cups prepared sushi rice
- ounces pickled ginger
- Wasabi (to taste)
- 4 sheets nori seaweed
- 1 tablespoon water

For the mushrooms:

- 8 tablespoons soy sauce
- 2 tablespoons sugar
- 2 cups water
- 10 dried shiitake mushrooms

Servings: 8 pieces

Total time: 40 min

Instructions:

1. Begin by preparing the egg mixture: whisk together the eggs, rice wine, soy sauce, sugar, and salt. Heat the oil in a pan specifically designed for making omelets. Add in the egg mix and keep cooking until a firm, flat omelet is formed. Allow the omelet to cool, then slice it into strips (approximately 1/2 inch) wide.
2. Bring approximately 1 cup of water to a boil. Put the shiitake mushrooms, soy sauce, and sugar, and let them cook for at least 10 minutes. Drain the mushrooms using a sieve, then cut them into strips. Cut the surimi sticks in half lengthwise.
3. In a pan (no oil), lightly toast the sesame seeds until they turn a light brown color. Briefly toast the nori sheets in the same dry pan. Drain the pickled ginger. Combine the vinegar and water and moisten your hands with this mixture.
4. Place one nori sheet on a bamboo rolling mat and spread a quarter of the rice evenly over the nori, leaving about 1/2 inch of space at the top. Press the rice firmly and create a thin strip of wasabi, approximately 1/4 inch wide, slightly to the right of

the center of the rice. Add some of the mushrooms, surimi, omelet strips, and sesame seeds. Roll the sushi firmly using the bamboo mat. Moisten your fingertips with the vinegar water again and shape again the roll to ensure it is tightly packed. Slice the sushi roll into equal-sized pieces after dipping a sharp knife into the vinegar water. Repeat this process with the remaining ingredients.

5. Sushi should be served on a serving tray or individual plates with pickled ginger, soy sauce, and wasabi for dipping.

Chicken futomaki

Ingredients:

- 1/2 cup sushi rice
- 2 sheets of nori
- 1 chicken fillet (about 5.3 oz)
- 2-3 tablespoons vegetable oil
- 2 tablespoons sake
- 4 tablespoons soy sauce
- 2 tablespoons sugar
- 4 tablespoons mirin
- 1 chopped chili pepper
- 1/2 celery stalk

For serving:

- 2 teaspoons wasabi
- 1 small bowl of soy sauce

Servings: 8 pieces

Total time: 55 min

Instructions:

1. Prepare the rice according to my sushi rice recipe.
2. Slice the chicken into thin strips. Mix them in a bowl with the sake, soy sauce, mirin, and sugar.
3. Marinate in your fridge for at least 30 minutes.
4. Slowly fry the chicken pieces in a little oil until golden. Mix with the marinade and let it reduce slightly.
5. Briefly toast one side of the nori sheets in a pan until they start to brown. Place them on a bamboo mat and arrange the rice and chicken lengthwise on top. Finely chop the celery and chili pepper.
6. Roll each sheet tightly using the mat to create a solid roll. Press with your hands and cut the roll into 8 slices. Serve the wasabi and soy sauce separately.

4 ingredients futomaki

Ingredients:

- 10.6 ounces of sushi rice
- 2 sheets of nori seaweed
- 1.4 ounces of imitation crab (surimi)
- 2.8 ounces of tuna (or fresh salmon)
- 1.4 ounces of carrots
- 1.1 ounces of avocado
- as needed of wasabi

Servings: 12 pieces

Total time: 30 min

Instructions:

1. To prepare the futomaki, begin by preparing the sushi rice using the basic recipe.
2. While the rice cools, cut the vegetables and fish into ½ thick sticks and set them aside. Arrange a sheet of nori seaweed on the bamboo mat, preferably lined with plastic wrap.
3. Spread 5.3 ounces of rice onto the nori, leaving 0.78 inches of seaweed free at the top edge. Place a small amount of wasabi paste in the center (without overdoing it, as it is very spicy).
4. Then add the sticks of four different ingredients.
5. Roll the seaweed tightly using the mat, and you will see that the seaweed will stick to itself in the area you left free, securing the roll.
6. Once the roll is complete, cut it into 3 or 6 pieces, depending on how thick you want them to be. Your futomaki sushi is ready. Keep them in your fridge until ready to serve.

Vegan futomaki

Ingredients:

- 10.6 ounces of sushi rice
- 2 tablespoons of rice vinegar
- 2 tablespoons of sugar
- 2 pinches of sake
- 1 piece of kombu seaweed
- Nori seaweed
- 1 large carrot
- 1 zucchini
- 1 avocado
- Salt
- Lemon juice

Servings: 10 pieces

Total time: 40 min

Instruction:

1. Fill a large bowl with rice and rinse it under cold running water, allowing the water to flow over it. Rinse well until the water runs clear and drain thoroughly. This step is crucial for removing excess starch and should be done meticulously to ensure the recipe's success.
2. In a large pot with a thick bottom, whisk 2 cups of water and the rice. Bring to a boil and simmer over low flame, covered, for 10 minutes. Do not uncover during this time. Remove from the flame and let the rice rest, allowing it to absorb the remaining liquid, for approximately 10 minutes.
3. Meanwhile, in a small saucepan, gently dissolve 1 tsp of salt and 2 tbsp of sugar in the rice vinegar and sake over low heat, making sure not to let it boil. Add the kombu seaweed and stir well. Allow the mixture to cool, remove the kombu seaweed, and evenly distribute the liquid onto the still warm rice, which should be spread out on a flat surface (I recommend using a dampened sheet of parchment paper).
4. Top the rice with a moist cloth and let it cool completely.
5. Prepare the filling by peeling and cutting the carrot into thin, uniformly sized strips. Do the same for the zucchini. Remove the avocado's peel and pit, then slice it thinly and evenly. To prevent browning, sprinkle the avocado slices with lemon juice. Blanch the vegetables in salted water with a small amount of rice vinegar. Cook them until they are soft but still firm. Drain and set aside, reserving the cooking liquid for later use.

6. Briefly toast the nori seaweed sheets over a flame until they become crisp. Place the shiny side of the seaweed down on a bamboo mat. Moisten your hands with the reserved vegetable cooking liquid and spread the rice evenly on the seaweed, creating a layer that is about 1/2 inch thick. Leave approximately 1 inch of seaweed uncovered at the edges.

7. Arrange the vegetables and avocado in the center of the rice, creating a harmonious combination of flavors. Using the bamboo mat, roll up the ingredients tightly, starting from the longer side. It's important to apply firm pressure to compact the seaweed and prevent the rice from spilling out.

8. For better results, wrap the rolled sushi tightly in plastic wrap and put it in the fridge for at least 1 hour before cutting. If possible, allow it to chill for half a day to make the slicing process easier.

9. When ready to serve, place the roll on a dry cutting board and use a sharp knife with a smooth blade to slice it into evenly sized cylindrical pieces. Serve the futomaki fresh and enjoy!

Chicken and avocado futomaki

Ingredients:

- 1 cup of sushi rice
- 1 cup of water
- 2 tablespoons of rice vinegar
- 1 tablespoon of sugar
- ¼ teaspoon of salt
- 1 chicken breast
- 4 tablespoons of soy sauce
- 2 tablespoons of mirin
- 2 tablespoons of sake
- 2 teaspoons of sugar
- 1 avocado
- 3 sheets of nori seaweed

Servings: 6 pieces

Total time: 50 min

Instructions:

1. In a big bowl, incorporate the ingredients for the teriyaki sauce and marinate the chicken strips for at least half an hour.
2. To begin, rinse the sushi rice under cold water, gently rubbing it with your hands until the water runs clear.
3. Allow the rice to soak in a bowl of water for 40 minutes.
4. Once soaked, transfer the rice and water to a pot.
5. Cover the pot with a lid (without a vent) and bring it to a boil over high heat. As soon as boiling, reduce the heat to low and let it simmer for approximately 12 minutes.
6. After removing the rice from the heat, leave its lid on for ten minutes without opening it to allow it rest.
7. In a glass, dissolve the sugar and salt in the rice vinegar.
8. Transfer the cooked rice to a non-metallic bowl and pour the vinegar mixture over it. Gently fold the rice with a wooden spatula, making long cuts to avoid breaking the grains.
9. Using a fan, cool the rice while continuing to gently mix it until it becomes glossy.
10. Bring the rice to reach the room temperature, covering it with a damp cloth.
11. In a preheated pan with a small amount of oil, cook the chicken strips from the marinade until almost done. Then, pour in the marinade and let it reduce until the sauce becomes sticky and thick. Remove from heat.
12. Peel and thinly slice the avocado.

13. Arrange a sheet of nori seaweed over a bamboo mat or use plastic wrap for easier rolling.
14. Moisten your hands with water each time you handle the rice and spread an even layer of rice onto the nori sheet, leaving 0.39 inches border at the opposite long end.
15. Arrange the avocado slices, cooked chicken strips, and optionally add mayonnaise.
16. Begin rolling the seaweed and mat from the bottom to the top, applying gentle pressure to ensure the filling is secure.
17. Seal the roll by pressing the edge without the filling.
18. With a sharp knife, cut the rolls into halves, then halve each piece again for bite-sized portions. Remember to wet the blade with water between cuts.

Uramaki recipes

Super colourful uramaki

Ingredients:

- 12 slices Avocado
- 4-piece Cucumber sliced lengthwise
- 3 cup Sushi Rice cooked
- 2 Nori Seaweed
- 8 slices Mango not too soft, rectangular
- 8 slices Avocado softer, rectangular
- 12-piece Surimi
- 8 slices Salmon raw and fresh, rectangular

Servings: 4 rolls

Total time: 15 min

Instructions:

1. Divide the nori sheet in half.
2. Spread most of the cooked rice onto the nori sheet, reserving 2 tablespoons. Distribute the rice evenly over the nori sheet and firmly press it down to ensure it adheres to the seaweed.
3. Flip the nori sheet with rice and apply the remaining rice to the surface. Leave approximately 1 inch of space at the top border and approximately ½ inch at the bottom. Ensure that the rice sticks to the nori sheet.
4. Prepare your filling ingredients. Have sliced avocado and cucumber ready.
5. Position the surimi pieces on the rice line so that they fit snugly. If necessary, cut the central surimi stick to fit properly.
6. Arrange the avocado and cucumber in the same manner.
7. Commence rolling the sushi using the sushi mat, applying pressure as you roll. This will ensure a tightly rolled sushi that remains intact when sliced.
8. Prepare your topping ingredients. Cut the salmon, mango, and avocado into thin slices approximately 0.1 inches thick, creating rectangular pieces.
9. Place the salmon, mango, and avocado slices on top of the sushi roll.
10. Cover the rainbow roll with plastic wrap and place the sushi mat over it. Apply pressure to ensure the toppings adhere to the cooked sushi rice.
11. Remove the plastic wrap and mat. Cut the sushi roll into 4 equally sized pieces.
12. Serve with soy sauce, wasabi, and slices of pickled Japanese ginger. Enjoy!

Classic California uramaki

Ingredients:

- 6 pcs Surimi aka imitation crab
- 2 sheets Nori Seaweed
- 1 cup Sushi Rice cooked
- ½ Avocado
- 2 Tablespoon Sesame Seeds
- 1 Cucumber
- 4 Tablespoon Japanese Mayonnaise

Servings: 2 rolls

Total time: 15 min

Instructions:

1. Slice the avocado into thinner pieces. Peel the cucumber and halve it lengthwise.
2. Position the nori seaweed on the sushi mat. Utilize a plastic-wrapped sushi mat to prevent the sushi from sticking.
3. Spread approximately half of the cooked rice (reserving about 2-3 tablespoons) evenly across the entire surface of the nori seaweed. Ensure that the rice completely covers the seaweed and forms a uniform layer.
4. Rotate the rice-covered seaweed and distribute the reserved 2-3 tablespoons of rice over one half of the seaweed, leaving about 1 inch from the bottom edge of the seaweed. Spread the rice to create an even layer.
5. Create a line of mayonnaise in the center of the rice.
6. Place one cucumber half over the mayonnaise and arrange 3 slices of avocado in a single line on top of it.
7. Position 3 surimi sticks in the center, forming a line.
8. Hold the seaweed with toppings and the plastic-wrapped mat, using both hands, and begin rolling the sushi.
9. Continue rolling the sushi, applying pressure with both hands to create a tightly wrapped roll. Roll until you have a compact sushi roll.
10. Place the sushi roll on one side of the mat and sprinkle sesame seeds over the remaining area of the mat.
11. Roll the sushi roll so that the inside-out portion collects the sesame seeds, completely covering the roll.
12. Remove the sushi from the bamboo mat and slice it into pieces about 1 inch thick, resulting in 8 thick slices.
13. Arrange the California roll on a plate and enjoy with soy sauce, wasabi, and pickled ginger slices as dipping options.

Avocado-based uramaki

Ingredients:

- 6 Tablespoon Japanese Mayonnaise
- 6-12 slice Cucumber cut lengthwise
- 3 sheet Nori Seaweed
- 3 Avocado
- Tobiko Fish Roe optional
- 4.5cup Sushi Rice cooked
- 12-piece Shrimp medium, cooked
- 18 slice Avocado

Servings: 6 rolls

Total time: 20 min

Instructions:

1. Ensure that the filling ingredients are prepared and ready. Cook and prepare the sushi rice, boil the shrimp for 5 minutes, slice the cucumber lengthwise, and cut the avocado into smaller pieces.
2. Divide the nori seaweed into two equal parts. We will only need half of it.
3. Spread the majority of the rice (keeping about 2-3 tablespoons aside) onto one side of the nori seaweed. Press it onto the nori sheet to create an even layer.
4. Flip the sheet with the rice and spread the remaining 2-3 tablespoons of rice onto the inner part of the nori sheet as well. Leave a border of about ½ to 1 inch at the top and bottom without adding rice.
5. Create a line of mayo over the rice and place the shrimp, cucumber, and avocado slices over the rice, ensuring they fit within the designated space. If necessary, trim the cucumber or avocado to ensure equal distribution.
6. Begin rolling the sushi using the bamboo mat. Roll gently and apply pressure with both hands to create a tightly wrapped sushi roll.
7. Slice the avocado half into thin pieces, preferably using a sharp knife.
8. Arrange the avocado slices over the sushi roll, spacing them out slightly to resemble green dragon scales.
9. Cover the avocado and the sushi mat with cling wrap, pressing it around the avocado to adhere to the inside-out sushi rice. The avocado slices should stick to the rice on the sushi roll.
10. Slice the sushi roll into 8 pieces using a sharp and clean knife. It's helpful to clean and moisten the knife after each cut.
11. If desired, top with tobiko fish roe and serve.

Spicy salmon uramaki

Ingredients:

- 2 sheets Nori Seaweed
- 1 Tablespoon Japanese Mayonnaise
- 2 cups Sushi Rice cooked
- ½ Avocado
- 4 Tablespoon Sesame Seeds white, black
- 1 filet Salmon fresh
- 1 Tbs Sriracha Sauce or another hot sauce to your liking

Servings: 2 rolls

Total time: 15 min

Instructions:

1. Ensure that all the ingredients are prepared and ready. Cook and prepare the sushi rice. Cut the avocado into 8 pieces and slice the salmon into 3 pieces. Cut one of the 3 slices in half.
2. Create spicy mayo by combining mayonnaise with sriracha. It is best to transfer the spicy mayo into a squeeze bottle for easy pouring in a straight line over the sushi rice later.
3. Place the nori seaweed on the sushi mat. Use a sushi mat wrapped in plastic to prevent the sushi from sticking.
4. Spread nearly half of the cooked rice (reserving about 2-3 tablespoons) evenly over the surface of the nori seaweed. The rice should cover the entire seaweed sheet and form a smooth layer.
5. Flip the rice-covered seaweed over and spread the reserved 2-3 tablespoons of rice on one half of the seaweed, leaving about a 1-inch gap from the bottom edge. Spread it out evenly.
6. Pour the spicy mayonnaise in a straight line at the center of the rice.
7. Place 1½ slices of salmon on top of the mayo line.
8. Arrange 4 avocado slices (2 larger and 2 smaller) over the salmon.
9. Bring the seaweed sheet with the toppings to the edge of the plastic-wrapped mat. Hold it with both hands and begin rolling the sushi.
10. Continue rolling the sushi while pressing down with both hands to create a tightly wrapped roll. Keep rolling until you have a compact sushi roll.
11. Position the sushi roll on one side of the mat and sprinkle sesame seeds over the rest of the mat.
12. Roll the sushi again so that the inside-out sushi roll picks up the sesame seeds and becomes completely coated with them.

13. Remove the sushi from the bamboo mat and slice it into 1-inch-thick pieces, resulting in 8 thick slices.
14. Place the salmon roll on a plate and enjoy it with soy sauce, wasabi, and pickled sliced ginger for dipping options.

Shrimp and avocado uramaki

Ingredients:

- 2 Cucumber cut into 2 slices in the length
- 4 sheet Nori Seaweed
- 4 cup Sushi Rice cooked
- 12 pieces shrimp small to medium sized
- 4 Tablespoon Mayonnaise
- 1.33 cup Tobiko Fish Roe
- 2 Avocado cut into 3 slices in the length

Servings: 4 rolls

Total time: 20 min

Instructions:

1. Have the cooked sushi rice prepared and ready.
2. Slice the half avocado lengthwise into 3 thin pieces. Peel and cut the cucumber in half lengthwise.
3. Butterfly the shrimp by splitting it open and removing the tail. Cook the cleaned shrimp in boiling water for 2-3 minutes.
4. Place the nori seaweed on the sushi mat. Use a sushi mat wrapped in plastic to prevent the sushi from sticking.
5. Spread almost all of the cooked rice (keeping about 2-3 tablespoons aside) evenly over the nori seaweed. The rice should completely cover the seaweed, forming a smooth and even layer. Use your fingers to press the rice onto the nori.
6. Flip the rice-covered seaweed over and spread the reserved 2-3 tablespoons of rice on one half of the seaweed, leaving about a 1-inch gap from the bottom edge. Spread it out evenly.
7. Spread a line of mayonnaise in the center of the rice.
8. Place the cooked shrimp and cucumber over the mayonnaise and arrange the 3 avocado slices on top in a single line.
9. Bring the seaweed sheet with the toppings to the edge of the plastic-wrapped mat, hold it with both hands, and begin rolling the sushi.
10. Continue rolling the sushi while pressing down with both hands to create a tightly wrapped roll. Roll until you have a compact sushi roll.
11. Add tobiko on top of the sushi roll as a topping.
12. Press down with another sushi mat to shape the roll and make sure that the tobiko sticks to the sushi.
13. Remove the sushi from the bamboo mat and cut it into 1-inch-thick slices, resulting in 4 thick slices.

14. Place the roll on a plate and enjoy it with wasabi and soy sauce for dipping options, along with some pickled sliced ginger.

Asparagus and salmon uramaki

Ingredients:

- 4 tablespoons roasted sesame seeds
- 4 ounces sashimi-grade salmon, cut
- ½ avocado, cut
- 4 asparagus stalks, trimmed and rinsed
- 2 whole nori sheets
- 2 tablespoons salmon roe
- Soy sauce
- 4 tablespoons roasted sesame seeds
- 1 teaspoon wasabi

Servings: 12 pieces

Total time: 30 min

Instructions:

1. Microwave the damp asparagus on a microwave-safe plate, covering it, for approximately 40 seconds until it becomes tender.
2. A sheet of nori should be placed on top of the makisu (a bamboo sushi mat) with its shiny surface facing up. Over the nori, distribute 1 cup of sushi rice in a uniform layer.
3. Sprinkle 2 tablespoons of sesame seeds onto the rice.
4. Take a piece of plastic wrap or parchment paper, similar in size to the makisu, and place it on top of the rice. Flip the makisu so that the nori side is facing upwards.
5. Arrange 2 asparagus stalks across the center of the nori. Below the asparagus, place half of the salmon and half of the avocado.
6. Begin rolling the sushi tightly by lifting the edge of the makisu and nori closest to you. Roll it over the filling, forming a compact jelly roll. Allow the roll to rest, seam-side down, at room temperature for 5 minutes. Repeat the process to create another roll using the rest of the nori, rice, sesame seeds, and filling.
7. Slice each sushi roll into 6 pieces. Place a small mound of wasabi in one corner of a serving plate and add ½ teaspoon of salmon roe to each sushi piece. Serve with individual small, shallow dishes of soy sauce for each person.

Spicy shrimp uramaki

Ingredients:

- 2 whole nori sheets
- 2 cups Sushi Rice
- 4 tablespoons roasted sesame seeds
- 2 tablespoons spicy mayonnaise sauce, divided
- 4 medium or large tail-on shrimp, deveined
- 1 tablespoon cornstarch
- ½ cup shredded red cabbage
- Sweet Eel Sauce
- ½ cup store-bought crispy fried onions
- Vegetable oil, for frying
- Tempura Batter
- 1 baby cucumber, cut
- ½ cup bean sprouts, washed

Servings: 12 pieces

Total time: 40 min

Instructions:

1. Create small incisions vertically along the underside of the shrimp, place them belly-side down on a cutting board, and gently press them to straighten. Coat the shrimp with cornstarch.
2. In a pan, warm about 2 inches of vegetable oil over medium heat until it glistens. Dip the shrimp into the batter, then fry them for around 2 minutes, flipping occasionally, until they turn golden. Transfer the fried shrimp to a wire rack to drain excess oil.
3. Arrange a layer of nori over the makisu with the glossy side facing down. Distribute an even layer of 1 cup of rice over the nori and sprinkle it with 2 tablespoons of sesame seeds. Top the rice with a piece of plastic wrap or parchment paper that is about the same size as the makisu, then flip the makisu so that the nori side is facing upwards.
4. Spread approximately ½ tablespoon of the mayonnaise sauce in the center of the nori. Position 2 shrimp, with their tails protruding from the nori, on top of the sauce. Arrange 2 cucumber sticks, ¼ cup of sprouts, and ¼ cup of cabbage below the shrimp.
5. Begin rolling the sushi tightly by lifting the edge of the makisu and nori. Roll it into a compact jelly roll. Allow the roll to rest, seam-side down, at room temperature for 5 minutes. Repeat the process to create another roll using the remaining nori, rice, sesame seeds, and filling.

6. Cut each sushi roll into six pieces and garnish each piece with a touch of the mayonnaise sauce, a drizzle of the eel sauce, and a sprinkle of fried onions.

Fried mozzarella uramaki

Ingredients:

- Vegetable oil, for frying
- 2 whole nori sheets
- 2 cups Sushi Rice
- 4 tablespoons roasted sesame seeds
- 3 mozzarella cheese sticks, halved
- 2 tablespoons all-purpose flour
- ½ cup Pico de Gallo (you can purchase it at any grocery store)
- Spicy Mayonnaise Sauce
- 1 egg, beaten
- ½ cup breadcrumbs
- 4 tablespoons roasted sesame seeds
- 1 romaine lettuce leaf, halved lengthwise

Servings: 6

Total time: 35 min

Instructions:

1. Coat the mozzarella sticks with a layer of flour, then by an egg wash, and finally, breadcrumbs.
2. In a pan, warm about 2 inches of vegetable oil over medium-high flame until it starts shimmering. Fry the coated mozzarella sticks, flipping them occasionally, until they turn golden, which usually takes around 30 to 60 seconds. Transfer the fried mozzarella sticks to a wire rack to facilitate any extra oil to drain.
3. A sheet of nori should be placed on top of the makisu with the shiny side facing down. Make sure the nori is completely covered by the sushi rice by spreading it out uniformly. Over the rice, scatter 2 teaspoons of sesame seeds. Arrange a piece of plastic wrap or parchment paper, similar in size to the makisu, on top of the rice and flip it so that the nori side is facing upwards.
4. Position a piece of lettuce in the center of the nori. Arrange 3 pieces of the fried mozzarella on top of the lettuce and spread ¼ cup of pico de gallo in a line below the mozzarella.
5. Begin rolling the sushi tightly by lifting the edge of the makisu and nori, creating a compact jelly roll. Allow the roll to sit for 5 minutes at room temperature. Repeat the process to create another roll using the rest of the nori, rice, sesame seeds, and filling.
6. Cut each sushi roll into six pieces, and drizzle them with mayonnaise sauce before serving.

Vegetarian uramaki

Ingredients:

- 2 cups Sushi Rice
- 4 tablespoons roasted sesame seeds
- 1 romaine lettuce leaf, halved lengthwise
- 1 baby cucumber, cut
- 1 tablespoon toasted sesame oil
- ½ yellow bell pepper, sliced
- 1 avocado, cut
- Finely ground Himalayan pink salt
- ½ cup Pickling Liquid
- 2 whole nori sheets
- ½ cup shredded red cabbage

Servings: 6

Total time: 50 min

Instructions:

1. Warm the sesame oil in a pan over medium-high flame until it starts to shimmer. Put the diced bell pepper and cook for approximately 5 minutes. In a mixing bowl, combine the cooked bell pepper with the pickling solution. Allow it to sit at room temperature for 20 minutes.
2. Arrange the makisu on a flat surface and put a sheet of nori on top, with the shiny side facing down. Distribute an even layer of 1 cup of sushi rice over the nori. Sprinkle 2 tablespoons of sesame seeds onto the rice. Top the rice with a piece of plastic wrap or parchment paper that is about the same size as the makisu. Flip the nori side up.
3. Position a piece of lettuce horizontally across the center of the nori. Arrange 2 pieces of cucumber, ¼ cup of cabbage, and the other half of the pickled bell pepper on top of the lettuce.
4. Carefully roll the makisu and nori tightly, creating a compact jelly roll. Remove the plastic wrap and makisu, arrange the roll seam-side down, and half of the avocado slices in a row lengthwise on top of the roll. Top the roll with the wrap and hold it strongly to ensure the avocado sticks to the roll securely. Bring it to reach the room temperature. Utilize the extra nori, rice, sesame seeds, garnishing, to make another roll.
5. Slice each sushi roll into 6 pieces, sprinkle with a pinch of salt, and serve.

Bacon uramaki

Ingredients:

- 1 tablespoon butter or margarine
- 2 eggs, beaten
- 8 turkey bacon slices
- 8 asparagus stalks, trimmed
- 2 cups Sushi Rice
- 4 tablespoons roasted sesame seeds
- 2 whole nori sheets, halved

Servings: 6 pieces

Total time: 40 min

Instructions:

1. Cook the bacon in a dry nonstick pan. Move it to a plate with paper towels to absorb extra grease.
2. Using the same pan, cook the asparagus for approximately 5 minutes, flipping occasionally, until it becomes slightly tender. Transfer the cooked asparagus to a plate.
3. In the same pan, melt the butter. Put the beaten egg in and cook it for approximately a minute over a medium-low flame, stirring occasionally to form little curds. Turn off the flame and leave the pot alone.
4. Set a sheet of nori on top of the makisu with the glossy side facing down. Over the nori, equally distribute 1/2 cup of rice. On the rice, add 1 tablespoon of sesame seeds.
5. Top the rice with a piece of plastic wrap or parchment paper that is more or less the same size as the makisu. Flip the nori side up.
6. Position one piece of bacon horizontally across the center of the nori. Put 2 asparagus stalks on top of the bacon, followed by another piece of bacon.
7. Carefully roll the makisu and nori into a tight jelly roll, starting from the edge closest to you. Let it sit, seam-side down, for 2 minutes. Repeat the process to make three more rolls using the rest of the nori, rice, sesame seeds, and filling.
8. Cut each sushi roll into six pieces and top each piece with the cooked egg. Serve and enjoy.

Chicken uramaki

Ingredients:

- 1 tablespoon mirin
- 1 tablespoon toasted sesame oil
- 2 whole nori sheets
- 2 cups Sushi Rice
- 6 ounces boneless, skinless chicken thighs, sliced into ½-inch-wide
- strips
- 2 teaspoons peeled, grated fresh ginger
- ½ cup shredded red cabbage
- 2 scallions, white and green parts, trimmed
- Mayonnaise
- 2 tablespoons soy sauce
- 2 tablespoons cooking sake
- 2 cups Sushi Rice
- 4 tablespoons roasted sesame seeds

Servings: 6 pieces

Total time: 45 min

Instructions:

1. In a spacious mixing bowl, incorporate the chicken, ginger, soy sauce, cooking rice wine, and mirin. Stir until the chicken is thoroughly coated. Place the mixture in the refrigerator to marinate for a minimum of 15 minutes.
2. Warm the sesame oil in a saucepan over medium heat until it glistens. Put the marinated chicken to the pan and cook for 7 minutes, blending consistently, until the chicken is completely cooked.
3. Spread out the makisu (sushi rolling mat) on a work surface and lay a sheet of nori on top, ensuring that the shiny side faces down. Evenly distribute 1 cup of rice across the nori. Sprinkle 2 tablespoons of sesame seeds over the rice. Cover the rice with a sheet of plastic wrap or parchment paper that matches the size of the makisu, then carefully flip it over so that the nori side is facing up.
4. Place half of the chicken in a line across the center of the nori sheet, followed by half of the onion and ¼ cup of red cabbage beneath the chicken.
5. Roll the makisu and nori tightly into a compact jelly roll. Allow it to rest, seam-side down, for approximately 5 minutes at room temperature. Repeat the process to create another roll using the rest of the nori, rice, sesame seeds, and filling.
6. Divide each sushi roll into 6 pieces and sprinkle them with scallions. Drizzle a small amount of mayonnaise over the rolls and serve.

Zucchini based uramaki

Ingredients:

- ¾ cup breadcrumbs
- Vegetable oil, for frying
- 2 whole nori sheets, halved
- 2 cups Sushi Rice
- 1 zucchini, cut into ½-inch-thick sticks
- 3 tablespoons all-purpose flour
- 1 avocado, cut
- Freshly ground black pepper
- 1 egg, beaten
- ¾ (8-ounce) package cream cheese, sliced into ½-inch-thick sticks

Servings: 6 pieces

Total time: 50 min

Instructions:

1. Prepare the zucchini by coating it with flour, followed by dipping it in beaten egg, and finally coating it with breadcrumbs.
2. In a deep-frying pan, warm approximately 2 inches of vegetable oil over medium-high flame until it starts shimmering. Begin to fry the zucchini for approximately 2 to 3 minutes, until it turns a golden-brown color. Once fried, transfer the zucchini to a wire rack to drain off any excess oil.
3. Place the sushi rolling mat (makisu) on a flat surface and lay a sheet of nori on top, ensuring that the shiny side is facing down. Spread an even layer of ½ cup of rice on the nori. Arrange a sheet of plastic wrap or parchment paper, similar in size to the makisu, on top of the rice and gently flip it over so that the nori side is facing upwards.
4. Arrange 2 or 3 pieces of the fried zucchini in a row across the center of the nori. Add 1 or 2 pieces of cream cheese below the zucchini.
5. Carefully lift the edge of the makisu and nori, rolling it tightly into a compact cylindrical shape. Remove the plastic wrap and makisu, then place the roll seam-side down. Arrange one-quarter of the avocado slices lengthwise next to each other on top of the roll. Cover the roll again with the plastic wrap, applying slight pressure to ensure the avocado adheres well. Allow it to sit at room temperature for 5 minutes. Repeat the process to make three more rolls using the rest of the nori, rice, filling, and topping.
6. Cut each sushi roll into 6 equal pieces and drizzle them with ground black pepper. Serve and enjoy your delicious zucchini sushi rolls.

Crab and mango uramaki

Ingredients:

- Freshly ground black pepper
- Juice of ½ lemon
- 2 whole nori sheets, halved
- 4 ounces cooked crabmeat, coarsely trimmed
- 1 teaspoon sweet chili sauce
- ½ avocado, cut
- 1 cup Spicy Mango Sauce
- Salt
- 2 cups Sushi Rice

Servings: 6 pieces

Total time: 45 min

Instructions:

1. Combine the crabmeat, sweet chili sauce, salt and pepper, and lemon juice in a bowl, stirring until thoroughly mixed.
2. Arrange the sushi mat on a flat surface and put a sheet of nori on top, ensuring that the glossy side is facing down. Spread an even layer of ½ cup of rice over the nori. Apply a piece of plastic wrap or parchment paper of similar size to cover the rice, and gently flip it over so the nori side is facing up.
3. Spread a line of the crab mixture, approximately 2 tablespoons, across the center of the nori. Arrange 2 or 3 avocado slices on top of the crab mixture.
4. Carefully roll the mat and nori tightly, creating a compact roll. Repeat the process with the rest of the nori, rice, and filling to produce three more rolls.
5. Cut each sushi roll into six pieces and top them with the mango sauce before serving.

Philadelphia uramaki

Ingredients:

- 4 tablespoons roasted sesame seeds
- 4 ounces sashimi-grade salmon, cut
- 2 whole nori sheets, halved
- 2 cups Sushi Rice
- 2 teaspoons wasabi
- Soy sauce
- ¾ (8-ounce) package cream cheese, cut into ½-inch-thick sticks

Servings: 6 rolls

Total time: 40 min

Instructions:

1. On a flat surface, lay the sushi rolling mat and place a sheet of nori on top, ensuring the shiny side is facing downwards. Spread an even layer of ½ cup of sushi rice across the nori, making sure to cover it entirely. Drizzle 1 tsp of sesame seeds over the rice.
2. Take a piece of plastic wrap or parchment paper, about the same size as the rolling mat, and place it on the rice. Flip the nori over so that the rice-covered side is now facing upwards.
3. Arrange 3 slices of salmon in the middle of the nori, and position 1 or 2 cream cheese sticks below the salmon.
4. Gently lift the edge of the rolling mat and nori closest to you, and carefully roll it into a tight cylinder. Allow it to rest, seam-side down, for 2 minutes. Repeat this process to create three more rolls using the remaining nori, rice, sesame seeds, and filling.
5. Using a sharp knife, which you should wipe clean with a damp kitchen towel before each cut, slice each sushi roll into 6 equal pieces. Create a small mound of wasabi on one corner of a serving plate. Serve the sushi alongside individual shallow dishes of soy sauce as desired.

Finishing Touch

Now all that remains is to complete our beautiful dishes. Sushi is a colorful and delicate dish, but with a little extra attention to presentation, it can become a true work of art.

First, get yourself some simple trays that complement our sushi dishes well—perhaps white, black, or wooden-colored trays. Then, let your imagination run wild by using denser sauces you have available to create geometric or soft semicircular lines on the trays. Place your preferred sushi pieces on top, aiming for a harmonious and organized arrangement.

Now you can unleash a multitude of shapes and colors by incorporating fresh flowers of various types, leaves, twigs, or thinly sliced lemon or orange zest to create vibrant bursts of joy.

The options are truly endless. Give free rein to your creativity and adorn your table with numerous marvelous, colorful trays.

Storage

In the unlikely event that you have leftover sushi, you can preserve it as long as you follow a few simple rules. We know that these exquisite dishes are made with raw and cooked fish, so we need to consider different preservation times for each.

Firstly, it's important to note that the rice tends to deteriorate, and fresh fish can harbor bacteria. Therefore, it's crucial to preserve them properly. Let's see how:

Preserving in the refrigerator:

Ensure that the temperature of your fridge is strictly between 0°C and 4°C (32°F and 39°F). If it goes beyond this range, it can not only affect the taste and texture but also promote bacterial growth. Place the sushi pieces close together, recreating the original shape, wrap them tightly with plastic wrap to prevent air exposure, and store them in a container, preferably an airtight one. When stored this way, sushi with raw fish can last up to a maximum of 24 hours, while sushi with cooked fish can last up to a maximum of 48 hours.

Preserving in the freezer:

Personally, I don't recommend freezing sushi as it can completely alter the texture. However, if you want to preserve your leftover bites and cannot consume them within two days, you can freeze them. Keep in mind that freezing will only give you an extra day of margin. Follow the same procedure as for the fridge: reshape the sushi into its original form, cover it with plastic wrap, and place it in an airtight container. Be aware that there is a 100% chance of flavor and texture alteration, so it may not be as enjoyable as fresh sushi. When taking it out of the freezer, allow it to thaw for a few hours in the refrigerator and then at room temperature. Avoid using quick thawing methods like the microwave or hot water bath.

Checking for freshness:

Whether you take it out of the fridge or freezer, always perform the "smell test" to determine if the sushi is still edible. It should not have a strong fishy odor or emit a sour fragrance typical of spoiled food. If this is the case, discard it. Also, visually inspect the colors; they should not appear significantly different.

Here's what you need to remember when preserving your leftover sushi:

- Vegetables and shrimp will crumble once they reach room temperature.
- Avocado tends to darken, so it's best to remove it before preserving the sushi.
- Do not preserve sushi with added sauces.
- Fried items will lose their crispness and become soft.
- Rolls or bites wrapped in seaweed will cause the rice to become gummy, so be aware of this.

Chapter 3. Bonus

Vegetarian cookbook

Vegetarian hosomaki recipes

Avocado hosomaki

Ingredients:

- wasabi paste
- pickled sushi ginger
- 1.25 cups prepared sushi rice, room temperature
- 2 nori sheets
- soy sauce
- 1 ripe avocado

Servings: 2 people (6 rolls)

Total time: 30 min

Instructions:

1. Get a bowl of water handy to wet your hands as needed during the process.
2. If you prefer, you can cover your bamboo sushi mat with plastic wrap to make cleaning easier, although it's not necessary for making these avocado maki rolls.
3. Prepare your ingredients in advance.
4. To avoid the sushi rice from drying out, cover it with a moist kitchen towel.
5. For thin rolls, known as hosomaki, you'll need to cut the nori sheets in half. Trim nori seaweed sheets by splitting the longest side because they are not completely square.
6. Peel the avocado and slice it into thin strips, ensuring they are no thicker than ½ inch.
7. Let's assemble the sushi roll.
8. With the longer edge towards you, lay the nori half sheet close to the bottom of the bamboo mat. The rough side should be facing up, so the smooth, shiny side ends up on the outside of the roll.
9. Take approximately four heaped tablespoons of cooked rice and place it on the rough side of the nori, facing up.

10. Gently spread the rice across the nori from left to right, using wet hands, making sure to leave a strip of exposed nori about ½ inch wide at the top and a thin strip at the bottom.
11. If the rice starts sticking to your hands, wet them again, and continue adding more rice until you achieve an even and thin layer.
12. Arrange the avocado slices horizontally in the center of the rice, forming a line of avocado slices.
13. Let's roll the avocado sushi.
14. As you carefully roll the nori around the avocado to join it with the rice, raise the bottom edge of the sushi mat. Avoid squeezing too tightly. The top part of the seaweed should remain open. Dip your finger in water and run it along the exposed seaweed at the top.
15. Continue rolling the sushi, applying gentle pressure to seal it, but be careful not to let the avocado squeeze out. Allow the exposed nori at the top to fold over the outside of the roll as the rice sticks together.
16. Gently tighten the roll using the sushi mat.
17. Now it's time to cut the avocado roll.
18. Traditionally, hosomaki is cut into 6 equally sized pieces.
19. Grab a sharp knife and either immerse it in water or use a moist kitchen towel to clean it. Divide the sushi roll in half, then place the two halves next to one another to create three pieces. Clean the knife between slices or if it becomes sticky.
20. You should obtain 6 bite-sized pieces of sushi.
21. Arrange the avocado sushi rolls on a plate and enjoy them with a bowl of soy sauce for condiment, along with wasabi paste and pickled ginger.

Grilled asparagus hosomaki

Ingredients:

- 10.5 ounces sushi rice
- 1 tbsp mirin
- ½ tsp Wasabi Paste
- 0.18 ounces chives
- 1 tbsp Soy Sauce
- ½ tbsp rice bran oil
- 2 sheets Sushi Nori, cut into half

Servings: 4 rolls

Total time: 30 min

Instructions:

1. To start, prepare the sauce by combining all the seasonings in a bowl and set it aside.
2. In a saucepan, warm a small amount of oil and add the asparagus to sauté until they become nicely browned.
3. While the asparagus is still hot, toss them with the sauce on a dinner plate. Allow them to cool for a few minutes to absorb the flavors.
4. Place a bamboo mat on a clean surface.
5. Split the nori sheet in half along the drawn lines, then place one half on the bamboo mat's front with the textured side facing up.
6. Moisten your hand with water to prevent the rice from sticking. This will make it easier to handle the rice.
7. Take a handful of cooked rice (approximately the size of a lemon) and spread it thinly and evenly over the nori, leaving a 0.79 iches gap at the top edge to seal the roll.
8. Make an indentation in the center of the sushi rice, then arrange the ingredients in a horizontal row, side by side.
9. Carefully and evenly roll the nori around the fillings, using the bamboo mat to assist in shaping the roll. Roll away from yourself, applying firm pressure to ensure a tight seal.
10. Once the roll is complete, press down firmly on the mat to slightly compress the roll and maintain its shape.
11. Cut the two halves into three equal sections, resulting in six sushi rolls. To keep the rice from adhering and achieve clean cuts, wash, or rinse the knife with a moist towel after every single cut.
12. Serve the sushi rolls with soy sauce and wasabi paste, or any recommended sauces. Enjoy sushi ginger between rolls to cleanse the palate.

Squash hosomaki

Ingredients:

- 1/2 cup short-grain rice
- 2 sheets of nori seaweed (size: 8.3 x 5.9 inches)
- 5.6ounces butternut squash
- 2.8 ounces leeks
- 0.53 ounces rice vinegar
- 0.35 ounces wasabi
- Salt to taste

Servings: 6 pieces

Total time: 30 min

Instructions:

1. To prepare the vegetarian hosomaki, start by cooking the long-grain rice. Rinse it under cold running water and boil it in salted water for 9 minutes. Drain the rice and season it with rice vinegar, then let it cool down at room temperature. Make horizontal cuts in the leek using a knife and separate the layers. Set up a steamer with a basket lined with parchment paper.
2. Place the leek leaves in the steamer and steam them for 5 minutes with the lid on. Once cooked, transfer them to a plate to cool.
3. Meanwhile, cut the squash into 4 rectangles measuring 8.3 inches long and approximately 0.4 inches in width and height. Place the squash rectangles in the same steamer and steam them for 7 minutes. Allow the squash to cool after steaming.
4. Now, place the seaweed on the designated sushi mat and spread the rice on top, ensuring it reaches the edge of the shorter side and leaving about 0.4 inches of empty space on both longer sides. Press it firmly with your hands.
5. Apply a thin strip of wasabi in the center using your finger.
6. Arrange 4 leek leaves evenly over the rice, covering the entire surface, and then place 2 squash rectangles in the center. Roll the hosomaki tightly from the bottom, exerting pressure with your hands until the roll is well compacted.
7. Transfer it to a cutting board and slice it in half first, and then into 6 pieces.
8. Your vegetarian hosomaki is now ready to be served, optionally with soy sauce.

Vegetarian uramaki recipes

Exotic style uramaki

Ingredients:

- 1 mango, peeled and sliced
- 1-2 Tbsp sesame seeds (optional)
- 1 cup smoked carrot "salmon" slices
- 4 sheets of nori, broken or cut in half
- Sushi rice
- 1 half seedless cucumber, peeled and thinly sliced
- ¼ cup Panko crumbs
- 1 avocado, sliced
- Chives (green tops of scallions or green onions)
- Spicy mayo (optionsl)
- Ginger, wasabi, soy sauce (optional)

Servings: 6 rolls

Total time: 40 min

Instructions:

1. Prepare a sushi mat or a piece of stiff paper by wrapping it tightly with a long piece of plastic wrap, ensuring the edges are neatly sealed.
2. Take a half sheet of nori and place it on top of the plastic-wrapped mat with the shiny side facing down.
3. Keep a small bowl of water with a damp paper towel nearby.
4. Use the water from the paper towel to wet your fingertips, then evenly distribute about a half cup of sushi rice over the nori sheet.
5. If desired, sprinkle with sesame seeds.
6. Carefully turn the nori over so that the rice and sesame side is now facing down.
7. Leave about half an inch of space from the edge and arrange a line of mango, avocado, carrot, cucumber, and chive from end to end. The roll must be carefully wrapped up, so take care not to overfill it.
8. Sprinkle 1 tablespoon of panko crumbs over the filling.
9. Using both hands and the sushi mat, start rolling the sushi from the bottom, making sure to tuck in the edge to fully enclose the filling.
10. Continue rolling until you reach the end, using the mat to help create an even and tightly rolled sushi.
11. Dampen the edge of a sharp knife with the damp paper towel.
12. Slice the sushi roll into 6 equal pieces by first cutting it in half, and then cutting each half into thirds.

13. Remember to wipe the knife with the damp paper towel between each cut to prevent the rice from sticking.
14. Arrange the sushi pieces on a serving dish and serve with pickled ginger and wasabi for added flavor.

Spicy vegan uramaki

Ingredients:

- 4 seaweed paper/nori
- 2 tablespoons rice vinegar
- 1 small avocado, sliced
- 2 tablespoons sugar
- 4 cups cooked sushi rice
- 1 large Jalapeno, seed removed and thinly sliced lengthwise (optional)
- 2 tablespoons apple cider vinegar
- 1.5 teaspoons salt
- ½ English cucumber, cut lengthwise into 8 strips
- Seaweed flakes (optional)

Servings: 4 rolls

Total time: 30 min

Instructions:

1. Combine apple cider vinegar and rice vinegar in a small bowl. Warm the mixture in the microwave for 10-15 seconds. Remove it from the microwave and dissolve sugar and salt into the vinegar.
2. In a large mixing bowl, blend the cooked sushi rice with the vinegar mixture. Ensure that the rice is evenly seasoned by mixing it well. Bring the rice to reach the room temperature if it is still warm.
3. Cover both sides of your sushi mat entirely with plastic wrap.
4. Place a sheet of seaweed on top of the wrapped sushi mat.
5. Spread approximately one cup of seasoned sushi rice onto the seaweed sheet, making sure to leave about an inch of the seaweed uncovered at the top.
6. If desired, sprinkle seaweed flakes over the rice and gently press them into the rice.
7. Grasp the top portion of the seaweed sheet and carefully flip it towards yourself, revealing only the seaweed without the rice. The bottom part of the seaweed should not show any rice when flipped.
8. Near the bottom part of the seaweed sheet, add the cucumber, avocado, and, if preferred, thinly sliced jalapeno for a slight heat and added crunch.
9. Hold the bottom part of the seaweed sheet and roll it over the ingredients, using the sushi mat to tightly roll everything together. The plastic wrap will avoid the rice from clinging to the mat. Take your time to ensure a tight roll.
10. Once the roll is complete, place it on a serving dish with the seam side facing down.
11. Continue making additional rolls using the same process.
12. Garnish the sushi roll with soy sauce or pickled ginger after being cut into bite-sized pieces.

Tofu uramaki

Ingredients:

- 3 Tbsps vegan mayo
- 2-3 avocados, cut into strips
- 1 cup sushi rice
- Nori sheets
- 2 cups water
- 1 tsp salt
- 3 Tbsps rice vinegar
- 1 Tbsp sugar
- Sesame seeds
- Silken tofu, cut into sticks
- Soy sauce or tamari for dipping

Servings: 6 rolls

Total time: 45 min

Instructions:

1. Start by thoroughly washing the rice until the water runs clear.
2. Transfer the rinsed rice to a pot, add the water, and bring it to a boil. Allow it to cook for 10 minutes once it reaches boiling point, then remove it from the heat. Cover the pot with a lid and let the rice absorb all the liquid.
3. In a mixing bowl, combine vinegar, sugar, and salt, stirring until fully dissolved. Pour the mixture into the rice and mix well to ensure even seasoning.
4. To cool the rice quickly, you can place it in the freezer or refrigerator, stirring every 5 minutes to speed up the process.
5. Prepare the avocado and tofu by cutting them into strips.
6. Cover a sushi mat with plastic wrap.
7. The coarse part of the nori sheet should be facing up and placed on top of the sushi mat. Over the nori sheet, evenly distribute a thin layer of rice and cover all the sides.
8. Sprinkle sesame seeds over the rice.
9. Top the rice with another layer of plastic wrap and gently turn it over. California rolls should have the rice, not the nori sheet, on the outside.
10. Remove the upper layer of plastic wrap from the nori sheet.
11. Spread a layer of vegan mayo onto the nori sheet, then place the avocado and tofu at the bottom of the sheet. Roll the sushi carefully.
12. Slice the vegan California roll using a knife dampened with water.
13. Enjoy with soy sauce and sesame oil for dipping.

Vegetarian futomaki recipes

Futomaki with veggies mix

Ingredients:

- Soy sauce
- Pickled ginger
- 1/2 avocado
- 1/2 cucumber
- 1/3 red pepper
- 1/3 yellow bell pepper
- 1/3 orange bell pepper
- 6 steamed asparagus
- Nori
- Wasabi
- 1 batch prepared sushi rice

Servings: 6 rolls

Total time: 35 min

Instructions:

1. Start by cutting your assortment of vegetables into long, slender pieces and store them in the refrigerator until you're ready to use them. Then, prepare the sushi rice according to your preferred method.
2. Next, place a sheet of seaweed on a clean surface and layer it with the rice. Using moistened hands, gently press down on the rice to create an even layer, leaving a clear margin of about an inch at one end.
3. Arrange the vegetable batons a few inches away from the rice, opting for visually appealing combinations that also offer a range of flavors.
4. Employ the sushi mat to firmly compress the ingredients together and tightly roll up the sushi.
5. Utilize both hands to apply consistent pressure, resulting in a compact roll that can be sliced easily without losing its form. With practice, you'll perfect the technique and may choose to fold the mat behind the roll as you proceed.
6. Serve the sushi alongside wasabi, pickled ginger, and soy sauce for dipping, enhancing the flavors and offering a delightful dining experience.

Tofu futomaki

Ingredients:

- 2 cups sushi rice
- Thinly sliced carrot (from 1 medium carrot)
- 4 sheets of nori seaweed
- 4 strips of pickled daikon
- 1 sliced avocado
- 4 strips pre-cooked kanpyo (gourd strips)
- 1.5 tablespoons of sugar
- ¼ cup rice vinegar
- 1 cucumber
- 1 teaspoon of salt
- ½ block of smoked tofu

Servings: 8 rolls

Total time: 50 min

Instructions:

1. Start by cooking the sushi rice in your rice cooker, using 2 cups of rice and the appropriate amount of water.
2. Prepare the fillings by slicing them into thin strips, making sure they are suitable in length for the nori sheets.
3. Set up your workspace, arranging the nori sheets, sushi rice (covered to keep it moist), and the prepared fillings.
4. Take a bamboo sushi rolling mat and place a nori sheet on top, ensuring that the smooth side is facing down. Position it closest to you for easier rolling.
5. Moisten your hands with the vinegar water mixture, then take a quarter portion of the rice and gently spread it onto the nori sheet. Leave a small, uncovered section at the top, around 0.78 inches in size.
6. Arrange the fillings on the nori sheet, starting with the sturdier ingredients at the bottom to facilitate smooth rolling.
7. With your thumb and index finger to keep together the mat and rice, and your other fingers to hold the fillings, roll the ingredients away from you in one fluid motion, applying firm pressure as you go.
8. Lift the bamboo mat, roll again, and firmly squeeze the roll. Repeat until you reach the top.
9. Make sure the bamboo mat fully covers the roll and give it a final gentle yet firm squeeze.
10. Remove the mat, then use a sharp knife to cut the roll straight down the middle.
11. To stop the rice from clinging, clean the knife with a moist towel after each cut.

Mushrooms futomaki

Ingredients:

- Soya sauce
- 2 sheets of Nori
- 1 cup Japanese rice
- 1 tsp salt
- 1/3 cup rice vinegar
- 1 1/2 tsp sweetener (sugar/honey)
- Bamboo mat for Sushi rolling
- Sesame seeds (for garnish)
- 1/3 cup shredded carrots (or Julienne cut)
- 1 avocado (thinly sliced)
- 1/3 cup thinly sliced mushrooms
- 1/3 cup Julienne cut cucumber/zucchini

Condiments

- 1/3 cup light soya sauce
- 2 tsp lemon juice
- 2 tsp sweetener (sugar)
- Wasabi Paste

Servings: 6 rolls

Total time: 30 min

Instructions:

1. Prepare the Japanese rice by cooking it with a slightly increased amount of water to achieve a sticky consistency. In a small bowl, incorporate the rice vinegar, sweetener, and seasoning, stirring until well mixed. Incorporate this mixture into the rice, ensuring even distribution, and set aside.
2. Partially cook the firm vegetables, such as carrots, by briefly boiling them. Set the vegetables aside. A bamboo sushi rolling mat should be covered with a layer of plastic wrap for hygiene before a sheet of nori is placed on it. Dampen your hands to prevent sticking. Using your hands, distribute a thin layer of rice evenly onto the Nori sheet, gently pressing it down.
3. Arrange the vegetables in a line along the center of the rice layer. Lift the edge of the mat and carefully roll it over the ingredients, applying a light but firm pressure. Roll the mat forward to complete the roll. Repeat the process with the remaining ingredients.
4. To slice the sushi roll, use a sharp knife that has been moistened to avoid rice from clinging. Slice the roll into 4 to 6 pieces.

Vegetarian udon recipe

Easy udon soup with veggies mix

Ingredients:

- 1 chopped scallion
- 1 head baby bok choy, halved
- 1 teaspoon freshly grated ginger
- 1 teaspoon minced garlic clove
- 1/2 cup sliced mushrooms
- 2 cups vegetable broth
- 2 tablespoons white miso paste
- 2 teaspoons divided toasted sesame oil
- 2-3 ounces fresh udon noodles
- 3 tablespoons divided soy sauce (plus more to taste)
- 3-4 chopped asparagus spears

Servings: 1 portion

Total time: 20 min

Instructions:

1. Warm a saucepan over medium-high flame and add 1 teaspoon of sesame oil. Cook the asparagus for about 2-3 minutes until it becomes soft when pierced with a fork. In the last minute of cooking, drizzle 1 tablespoon of soy sauce. Remove the asparagus from the pan and set it aside.
2. Then, add the final teaspoon of sesame oil to the saucepan and cook the mushrooms for an additional two to three minutes. During the last minute, incorporate 1 tablespoon of soy sauce. The mushrooms should be removed from the saucepan and placed aside.
3. In a pot, incorporate the remaining tablespoon of soy sauce, miso paste, garlic, ginger, and vegetable broth. Place the pot over medium-high flame and bring the mixture to a gentle simmer, stirring until the miso paste dissolves completely.
4. Add the udon noodles and bok choy to the pot and simmer for at least 2-3 minutes until the noodles are cooked. Taste the broth and adjust the flavor by adding more soy sauce if desired. Transfer the prepared dish to a bowl and garnish it with scallions.

Vegetarian rice noodles recipe

Vegetarian noodles with a touch of maple syrup

Ingredients:

- Salt and black pepper (to taste)
- 1 medium zucchini, sliced
- 1 large carrot, sliced
- 3-4 garlic cloves, minced
- 1/2 heaped tbsp fresh ginger, grated
- 8 oz rice noodles
- 7 oz fresh mushrooms, chopped
- 3/4 tsp onion powder
- 1 tbsp (sesame) oil
- 1 red bell pepper, sliced
- 1/2 tsp smoked paprika
- 1 tbsp cornstarch
- 2 tbsp rice vinegar
- 1 pinch of red pepper flakes optional
- 2/3 cup vegetable broth or water
- 2 tbsp maple syrup
- 3-4 tbsp tamari or soy sauce

Servings: 4 portions

Total time: 25 min

Instructions:

1. Prepare rice noodles in a pot of salted water until they reach a firm, yet tender texture (avoid overcooking).
2. Meanwhile, in a skillet or wok, heat up a drizzle of oil and sauté grated ginger and minced garlic over medium heat for approximately 2 minutes, ensuring to stir regularly. Incorporate the mushrooms, carrot, red bell pepper, zucchini, and the assortment of spices, sautéing for at least 5 minutes until the vegetables have softened. Maintain consistent stirring and consider adding a splash of water or vegetable broth to prevent scorching.
3. Vegetable broth, tamari, rice vinegar, maple syrup, cornstarch, and red pepper flakes should all be combined together easily for the sauce in a bowl while being properly whisked. Alternately, add the sauce's ingredients to a mason jar with a lid and give it a good shake.
4. Add the sauce to the saucepan and bring it to a simmer before serving. Give it a minute to simmer.

5. Incorporate the drained noodles into the skillet, tossing them together to ensure an even distribution of the sauce. Continue cooking for an additional 1-2 minutes. Take a taste and adjust the seasoning as desired by adding more salt, pepper, tamari, sweetener, or other preferred seasonings. For a creamier texture, consider incorporating a few spoonfuls of peanut butter.

6. Finalize the dish by garnishing it with minced green onions (scallions) and sesame seeds. Serve and savor the delightful flavors. Any leftovers can be kept in the fridge, covered, for up to 3 days.

Vegetarian Gyoza recipe

Vegan dumplings with potatoes

Ingredients:

- 5 shiitake Mushrooms
- ½ teaspoon Salt
- 25 sheets Gyoza Wrappers
- Sesame Oil
- 1 tablespoon Garlic Ginger Soy Sauce
- 1 tablespoon Potato Starch
- 1 clove Garlic
- 1 clove Ginger
- ¼ Cabbage
- ¼ bunch of Nira, garlic chives or scallions
- 1 2/3 cups soy sauce

Servings: 25 dumplings

Total time: 30 min

Instructions:

1. Finely chop nira and cabbage using a food processor until they are finely diced. Transfer the chopped vegetables to a bowl and mix them with salt, allowing them to sit for a duration of 10 minutes to enhance the flavors.
2. Utilize the same food processor to finely mince the shiitake mushrooms as well.
3. Once the time has elapsed, remove any excess moisture from the nira and cabbage mixture. Incorporate the minced shiitake mushrooms, potato starch, and a delectable sauce made from garlic and ginger into the bowl. Thoroughly combine all the ingredients until well mixed.
4. Take a gyoza wrapper and place it gently onto your palm. Spoon approximately 1 or 2 teaspoons of the prepared filling onto the center of the wrapper, and adeptly wrap it according to the instructions provided in the accompanying section.
5. In a frying pan, warm sesame oil over medium flame and carefully arrange the gyoza in a single layer, ensuring they have sufficient space to cook evenly.
6. Next, add ¼ cup of water to the pan, cover it with a lid, and allow the gyoza to steam for approximately 2 to 3 minutes, ensuring they become tender and flavorful.
7. Remove the lid, allowing any excess water to evaporate. Drizzle some sesame oil around the frying pan, enabling the gyoza to achieve a delightful golden-brown color. Continue cooking for an additional minute to attain the desired crispiness.
8. Once cooked, turn off the heat, place a plate over the gyoza, and skillfully invert the frying pan to effortlessly transfer the gyoza onto the plate.

9. To create a delicious sauce, finely mince garlic and ginger using the food processor.
10. Combine soy sauce, minced garlic, and minced ginger in a jar, thoroughly stirring to ensure all the flavors are well blended.
11. Store the jar in the refrigerator, and you can savor the flavorful sauce on the following day.

Delicacies: The most refined dishes

Spicy edamame

Ingredients:

- 1 Tbsp fresh ginger, finely trimmed or grated
- 2 cloves garlic, finely minced or grated
- 1 Tbsp coconut oil (oravocado oil)
- 1 Tbsp maple syrup
- 1 ½ Tbsp tamari
- 1/4 cup water
- 1/2 tsp toasted sesame oil
- 16 oz. frozen edamame in pods
- 1/2 tsp arrowroot starch
- Black pepper to taste

Servings: 4 portions

Total time: 30 min

Instructions:

1. Prepare the edamame according to the instructions on the packaging. You can choose to microwave them (covered), steam them, or boil them, as all methods yield equally satisfying results. In our case, the edamame was boiled in 0.75 gallons of salted water for 8 minutes before being drained and set aside.
2. In a tiny mixing bowl, blend water and arrowroot starch while the edamame is cooking.
3. Whisk the mixture until the starch is completely dissolved. Set it aside for later use.
4. After that, dissolve the coconut oil in a sizable non-stick or stainless-steel saucepan over a medium-low flame. Once melted, add the garlic, ginger, and black pepper. Sauté the ingredients for 1-2 minutes until they become fragrant and lightly sizzle. Be cautious not to let the garlic burn, as it can develop a bitter taste.
5. Now, add tamari and maple syrup to the skillet, stirring to ensure even distribution. Then, incorporate the arrowroot and water slurry into the mixture. Bring the combined ingredients to a boil, then reduce the flame and let them simmer for at least 2-3 minutes until the sauce thickens and becomes sticky.
6. Remove the saucepan from the flame and put the cooked edamame to the sauce, stirring well to coat them evenly. To get an extra touch of flavor, you can drizzle some toasted sesame oil (optional) over the dish and give it a final toss. Now it's ready to be enjoyed! This dish pairs wonderfully with stir-fries, fried rice, or noodles.

7. For the best taste, consume it while fresh. Any leftovers, though, can be kept in the fridge for two to three days. You may steam them in a pan with a lid or warm them in the microwave. Please be aware that this dish should not be frozen.

Miso soup with clams

Ingredients:

- 3 tablespoons red miso paste
- 3 cups water
- ⅓ cup canned clams
- 2 scallions, white and green parts, trimmed

Servings: 4 portions

Total time: 15 min

Instructions:

1. Heat a saucepan over medium heat and bring the water to a gentle boil. Introduce the clams into the simmering water and let them cook for 2 minutes.
2. Position a fine-mesh hand strainer with a diameter of 5 inches over the pan. With the aid of a spoon, carefully place the miso paste into the strainer, allowing it to dissolve into the soup while stirring occasionally. Once the miso paste has fully dissolved, turn off the heat and add the scallions to the skillet.
3. Transfer the flavorful soup into bowls specifically designed for miso soup or small soup bowls, ensuring a delightful presentation for serving.

Dragon cloud

Ingredients:

- Peeled shrimp 10.5 oz
- Tapioca flour 10.5 oz
- Salt, to taste
- Black pepper, to taste
- Sunflower seed oil, as needed

Servings: 4 portions

Total time: 1h30 min/ 13 hours rest of the dough

Instructions:

1. To prepare the Dragon Cloud, start by rinsing the shelled shrimp under running water and drying them with paper towels. Finely chop the shrimp and transfer the resulting puree to a bowl. Add tapioca flour and salt, and season with a touch of black pepper. The mixture should be massaged for roughly 10 minutes to produce a dough that is smooth and homogenized. If the dough is too dry, you can pour a small amount of water. Conversely, if it seems too moist, incorporate some additional tapioca flour.
2. Split the dough in half and shape each part into sausage-like rolls with a diameter of around 1.6 inches, ensuring there are no air bubbles present. Place the rolls in a steaming basket, cover with a lid, and steam over medium flame for one hour. Either a traditional steamer or a Chinese bamboo steaming basket can be used for this process.
3. Once cooked, allow the dough to cool, then fold it in plastic wrap and keep in the fridge for 12 hours. Alternatively, you can place it in the freezer for a couple of hours.
4. Next, slice the dough into very thin pieces. To get rid of any moisture, place the dough slices on a baking sheet covered with parchment paper and cook them in an oven at 140°F for an hour. Afterward, let the slices rest for an additional hour.
5. Heat sunflower seed oil in a skillet or wok. Once the oil reaches a temperature between 300°F and 350°F, immerse the slices in the oil until they become puffed up and crispy. Remove the chips from the oil with a spoon, letting any extra oil drip off, and set them on a baking tray covered with paper towels to soak up any leftover oil.
6. Serve the Dragon Cloud chips immediately. To fully savor their crispy texture, enjoy them right after frying, perhaps alongside some delectable dipping sauces.

Shrimp and veggies rice noodles

Ingredients:

- 12 oz shrimp
- 1 cup shredded carrots
- 1 tbsp tamari
- 1 egg
- 3 tbsp oyster sauce
- 1 tsp chili paste
- 3 stalks green onions
- 1 head broccoli
- 1 tbsp olive oil
- 8 oz flat rice noodles

Servings: 4 cups

Total time: 25 min

Instructions:

1. Prepare the flat rice noodles as directed on the packaging. Once cooked, drain them and set them aside.
2. Preheat a large skillet using avocado oil. Pour in tamari and cook the shrimp until they are no longer translucent, but instead turn a pink color on both sides. This process should take approximately 3-4 minutes. When cooked, remove the shrimps from the skillet and set them aside.
3. Add additional oil to the skillet and carefully crack the egg onto the pan. Cook the egg until it reaches a soft consistency. Remove the egg from the saucepan and put it aside with the cooked shrimp.
4. Pour more oil into the skillet and add the broccoli, carrots, and green onion stalks. Cook the vegetables until they become softened, which should take about 2-3 minutes. Stir in the oyster sauce to enhance the flavors.
5. Combine the cooked shrimp, egg, rice noodles, and desired amount of chili paste into the skillet with the cooked vegetables. Mix everything together until well combined.

Rice noodles with veggies and chicken

Ingredients:

- 1 tsp cornflour / cornstarch
- 6 oz chicken breast, sliced into thin strips
- 1 tsp oil
- 1/2 tsp each sesame oil, sugar (optional)
- 1 1/2 tbsp cooking wine
- 2 tbsp oyster sauce
- 1 tbsp dark soy sauce
- 1/4 tsp white pepper (you can also use black pepper)
- 3 tbsp water
- 1 small onion, sliced (white, brown, yellow)
- 1/2 greens, stems separated from leaves
- 1/2 red capsicum / bell pepper, sliced
- 3.5oz dried rice noodles
- 1 tbsp oil
- 1 garlic clove
- 1 carrot, sliced in half lengthwise and cut on the diagonal
- 5-7 mushrooms, sliced
- Sesame seeds
- green onions/scallions, chopped

Servings: 2 portions

Total time: 15 min

Instructions:

1. In a mixing bowl, incorporate the chicken, cornstarch, and oil, thoroughly mixing the ingredients together.
2. In another bowl, combine the ingredients listed from number 4 to number 9.
3. Just prior to cooking, follow the instructions on the noodle package to soak the noodles in hot water. Once soaked, drain them.
4. Heat up some oil in a large pan over medium- high heat.
5. Put the garlic and onion to the hot oil and cook for about 30 seconds.
6. Incorporate the chicken into the skillet and cook for approximately 1 minute until it transitions from pink to white in color.
7. Add the green stems, carrot, and capsicum to the skillet, and cook for another minute.
8. Introduce the mushrooms into the mixture and cook for an additional 30 seconds.
9. Add the soaked noodles, green leaves, and sauce to the skillet. Toss the ingredients for approximately 1 minute until the leaves have wilted and the sauce has

evaporated. Be cautious not to exceed 1 1/2 minutes of tossing, as it may cause the noodles to break.

10. To garnish, sprinkle sesame seeds and green onions over the dish. Serve immediately.

Traditional pork steamed dumplings

Ingredients:

- 3/4 cup bread flour
- 1/2 teaspoon salt
- 3/4 cup all-purpose flour
- 1/3-1/4 cup water (depending on the absorption of the flour)
- 1 piece of ginger (3/4 inch)
- 2 cloves of garlic
- 1/2 teaspoon salt
- lb ground pork
- 1/2 bunch fresh cilantro
- green onions
- 1/4 teaspoon pepper
- 1/2 tablespoon sesame oil
- 1 tablespoon soy sauce

Servings: 2 portions

Total time: 55 min

Instructions:

1. In a bowl, whisk 3/4 cup all-purpose flour and 3/4 cup bread flour.
2. Put 1/2 teaspoon of salt to the flour mixture and stir to combine.
3. Gradually add 1/3 to 1/4 cup of water, adjusting the amount as needed based on the absorption of the flour.
4. The ingredients should be combined well until a dough forms.
5. Move the dough to a spotless surface, then massage it for 5 to 7 minutes, or until it is elastic and smooth.
6. Create a ball out of the dough and wrap it in a fresh kitchen towel. 30 minutes of rest will help the gluten to rest.
7. While the dough is resting, begin preparing the filling. In a separate bowl, combine 1.1 lb ground pork, 1/2 bunch of fresh cilantro (chopped), 2 green onions (finely sliced), 1 piece of ginger (3/4 inch, grated), 2 cloves of garlic (chopped), 1/2 tsp of salt, 1/4 teaspoon of pepper, 1/2 tablespoon of sesame oil, and 1 tsp of soy sauce. To thoroughly incorporate all ingredients, stir well.
8. Split the dough into small parts after it has rested, and then roll each piece into a thin circle.
9. Spoon a small amount of the stuffing onto the center of each dough circle.
10. Fold the dough over the stuffing and press the edges firmly to seal the dumplings, creating a half-moon shape.

11. To create all the dumplings, continue the process using the leftover dough and filling.
12. Bring a saucepan of water to a boil, then add the dumplings to cook. When they rise to the surface and the stuffing is thoroughly cooked, cook for about 4-5 minutes.
13. With a slotted spoon, remove the cooked dumplings from the water and serve them hot with your preferred dipping sauce.

Veggie dumplings with spicy sauce

Ingredients:

- ¼ cup chopped green onions
- ¼ cup low-sodium soy sauce
- ⅓ cup rice vinegar
- ½ teaspoon crushed red pepper
- 2 cups all-purpose flour
- ⅔ cup water
- 2 teaspoons grated peeled fresh ginger
- 2 tablespoons chopped green onions
- ¼ teaspoon dark sesame oil
- 4 cups finely chopped green cabbage
- 3 garlic cloves, minced
- 2 tablespoons low-sodium soy sauce
- Cooking spray
- 2 tablespoons mirin (sweet rice wine)
- 4 cups diced shiitake mushroom caps (about 3/4 pound)
- ½ teaspoon salt
- 24 lettuce leaves
- 2 tablespoons peanut oil, divided

Servings: 12 portions

Total time: 50 min

Instructions:

1. To make the dipping sauce, incorporate ⅓ cup of rice vinegar, ¼ cup of finely chopped green onions, ¼ cup of low-sodium soy sauce, and ½ teaspoon of crushed red pepper flakes. Set the sauce aside for later.
2. For the dough, mix together ¾ cup of all-purpose flour, ¾ cup of bread flour, ½ teaspoon of salt, and ⅓ to ¼ cup of water (adjust the amount of water depending on the flour's absorption). The dough should be massaged on a floured surface and worked for 5 minutes. The dough should be covered and rested for 30 minutes.
3. In a large non-stick saucepan sprayed with cooking oil, heat it over medium-high heat. When the liquid has evaporated, add the mushrooms and simmer, stirring regularly, for about 3 minutes.
4. Adding the cabbage, simmer for a further 3 minutes, stirring constantly, until tender. Add 2 tablespoons of finely diced green onions, along with the sesame oil, ginger, garlic, salt, and soy sauce. The mixture should simmer for two minutes before being turned off and set aside. The dough should be cut into 4 equal pieces. Divide each rope into 12 equal pieces after rolling each half into a 1-inch-thick rope.

5. Mold each piece into a ball and roll it out into a 4-inch circle on a floured surface, keeping the circles covered with a damp towel to prevent drying.
6. Working with one wrapper at a time, spoon 2 teaspoons of the mushroom filling into the center of the wrapper. Fold it in half and create pleats along the top edge at ½-inch intervals, pressing it against the bottom edge to seal.
7. Warm a large non-stick pan over medium-high heat and add a small amount of oil. Place the dumplings in the skillet, pleated side up, and cook for about 2-3 minutes until the bottom turns golden brown.
8. Pour a small amount of water into the skillet, just enough to cover the bottom. Cover the saucepan with a lid and bring the flame to medium. Allow the dumplings to steam for about 8-10 minutes, or until the water has evaporated and the dumplings are cooked through.
9. The dumplings should simmer for an extra minute without the lid so that the bottoms can become crunchy. Continue the cooking procedure with the other dumplings, then move them to a plate.
10. Serve the dumplings with the prepared dipping sauce.

Soy noodles with veggies and shrimps

Ingredients:

- 1 lb Large Shrimp peeled and deveined
- 8 oz soy noodles
- 2-3 Green Onions thinly sliced
- 1 medium Carrot julienned or chopped
- 1 red bell pepper, sliced into strips
- 3 Garlic Cloves minced
- 2 Tbsp Toasted Sesame Seeds to garnish
- 1 Tbsp Olive Oil or peanut oil
- 3 Cups Broccoli Florets
- 1/4 Cup Fresh Orange Juice
- 2 Tsp Sesame Oil
- 1/4 Tsp Chili Flakes
- 2 Tbsp Raw Honey
- 1 Tsp Freshly Grated Ginger
- 2 Tbsp Hoisin Sauce
- 1/4 cup soy sauce or coconut amino

Servings: 4 portions

Total time: 30 min

Instructions:

1. In a large pot of vigorously boiling water seasoned with salt, cook the spaghetti following the instructions on the package.
2. During the final 2-3 minutes of cooking, introduce the broccoli florets into the pot and allow them to cook alongside the pasta until they reach a tender consistency. Drain the mixture, then keep it aside it. Soy sauce or coconut aminos, orange juice, honey, hoisin sauce, sesame oil, ginger, and chili flakes should be quickly incorporated together in a small dish.
3. Utilize a generous tablespoon of oil to heat up a capacious skillet over medium-high heat. Proceed to add the shrimp, garlic, and a sprinkle of salt and pepper.
4. Let the ingredients cook for a duration of 2-3 minutes, then introduce the carrots and bell pepper into the skillet and continue cooking for an additional minute or until the components are adequately heated.
5. Combine the cooked spaghetti and broccoli with the remaining ingredients in the skillet, followed by pouring the prepared sauce over the mixture. Toss everything together to ensure even distribution.
6. To complete the dish, embellish it with green onions and sesame seeds. Savor the delightful flavors!

Soy noodles with veggies and eggs

Ingredients:

- 1 bunch greens, trimmed, cut into 2" lengths, thick stalks halved
- 1 large red capsicum, sliced
- 4 eggs, lightly beaten
- 7oz sugar snap peas, trimmed, halved
- 1 long red chilli, deseeded, finely chopped, plus extra sliced chilli, to serve
- 1 tablespoon hoisin sauce
- 14oz soy noodles
- 2 teaspoons finely grated fresh ginger
- 1 tablespoon lime juice
- 1 medium red onion, sliced into wedges
- 1 tablespoon reduced-salt soy sauce
- 2 cloves garlic, crushed

Servings: 4 portions

Total time: 35 min

Instructions:

1. Combine tamari, oyster sauce, lime juice, and chili pepper in a petite bowl. Set aside. Cook the noodles following the instructions indicated on the package. Drain the noodles and put them aside.
2. Spritz a spacious wok lightly with olive oil and place it over high heat. Pour the beaten egg into the wok, tilting it to ensure the entire base is covered, creating a thin omelette. Allow the egg to cook for approximately 1 minute, or until it sets. Remove the omelette from the pan, roll it up, and slice it. Repeat this process to create a second omelette.
3. Spritz the wok with a small amount of oil. Stir-fry the onion for a duration of 2 minutes, or until it obtains a light golden hue. Put the ginger and garlic, and continue stir-frying for 30 seconds, or until the aroma becomes fragrant. Incorporate the bell pepper, sugar snap peas, and leafy greens, and continue stir-frying for 2 minutes, or until they reach a state of partial tenderness.
4. Introduce the reserved noodles and the prepared sauces to the wok, and stir-fry the mixture for 1-2 minutes, or until it is thoroughly heated. Serve the noodles promptly, garnishing them with the sliced omelette and additional chili slices.

Traditional ramen noodle soup

Ingredients:

- thumb-sized piece of ginger, sliced
- ½ teaspoon Chinese five spice
- pinch of chili powder
- 1 teaspoon white sugar
- 3 cups chicken stock
- 3 garlic cloves, halved
- 13.25ounces ramen noodles
- ounces sliced cooked pork or chicken breast
- 2 teaspoons sesame oil
- tablespoons soy sauce, plus extra to season
- 1 teaspoon Worcestershire sauce
- 4 boiled eggs, peeled and halved
- 1 sheet dried nori, finely shredded
- 3.5 ounces baby spinach
- 4 tablespoons sweetcorn
- sliced green spring onions or shallots
- sprinkle of sesame seeds

Servings: 4 portions

Total time: 35 min

Instructions:

1. In a large stockpot or saucepan, combine 3 cloves of garlic, cups of chicken broth, 4 tablespoons of soy sauce, 1 teaspoon of Worcestershire sauce, a sliced piece of ginger (about the size of a thumb), ½ teaspoon of Chinese five spice, a pinch of chili powder, and 10 fluid ounces of water. Bring the mixture to a boil and then reduce the flame to simmer for 5 minutes.
2. Taste the broth and adjust the flavor according to your preference by adding 1 teaspoon of white sugar or more soy sauce to make it sweeter or saltier.
3. Prepare 13 ounces of ramen noodles according to the instructions on the package. When cooked, drain the noodles, and put them aside.
4. Slice 14 ounces of cooked pork or chicken and sauté it in 2 teaspoons of sesame oil until it starts to brown. Set the cooked meat aside.
5. Divide the cooked noodles evenly into four bowls. Add a quarter of the chopped meat, 0.88 ounces of spinach, 1 tablespoon of sweetcorn, and two boiled egg halves to each bowl.
6. Return the broth to a clean skillet and bring it back to a boil.

7. Evenly distribute the hot broth among the four bowls. Garnish each bowl with shredded nori, chopped spring onions or shallots, and a pinch of sesame seeds. Allow the spinach to slightly wilt before eating.

Udon noodles with veggies and shrimps

Ingredients:

- 1 pack udon noodles preferably vacuum-packed
- 1 yellow onion, sliced
- white mushrooms, sliced
- 8-10 shrimp
- 1 spring onion green & white separately trimmed
- 1 carrot cut matchstick-style
- 1 garlic, chopped
- pinch salt and pepper
- 2 tablespoon neutral oil
- 1 tablespoon regular soy sauce
- 1 teaspoon brown sugar
- 1 tablespoon oyster sauce
- 1 teaspoon dark soy sauce
- 1 teaspoon rice vinegar
- 1 tablespoon toasted sesame oil
- pinch salt
- ⅓ teaspoon freshly crushed black pepper

Servings: 2 portions

Total time: 20 min

Instructions:

1. Boil the udon noodles following the instructions on the package. When the noodles are done, drain and rinse with cool water. Sprinkle a bit of oil over the noodles and set them aside.
2. Warm 1 tablespoon of oil in a pan and sauté the trimmed garlic for about 1 minute. Add the mushrooms and cook them on high heat until done. Then, add the onions, the white section of the spring onions, and the carrots. Stir-fry for 2-3 minutes. Remove the vegetables from the saucepan and sprinkle with salt and pepper.
3. Put 2 tablespoons of oil to the same saucepan and cook the shrimp. Put soy sauce and a bit of salt to taste. Sauté the shrimp until they become opaque.
4. Cook the udon noodles in the saucepan.
5. Stir-fry them on high heat, continuously tossing them to achieve a slight crispiness.
6. Pour the sauce over the noodles. Mix to equally cover the noodles with the sauce.
7. Add the sautéed vegetables to the skillet.
8. Turn off the heat and garnish with the green part of the spring onion.
9. Transfer the dish to a plate and enjoy!

Udon noodles with chicken

Ingredients:

- garlic cloves, trimmed
- 1 tablespoon soy sauce
- 1 tablespoon cooking sake
- 1 tablespoon cornflour
- 4 chicken thigh, boneless and skinless, cut into 1-inch strips
- 1 tablespoon fish sauce or lime juice
- 2 tablespoons sweet chilli sauce
- 1 tablespoon oyster sauce
- 1 tablespoon Sriracha
- ¼ cup hot water
- 1 cup cabbage, thinly sliced
- 1 bunch broccolini, roughly chopped
- black pepper, freshly cracked, a pinch
- 1/4 tsp white sesame seeds
- Flaky salt, to taste
- 3 garlic cloves, minced
- ½ cup spring onions, chopped (green only)
- 2 tablespoons grapeseed oil
- 9.52 oz raw udon noodles
- 1 red capsicum, deseeded, halved and cut into strips
- 1/4 tsp black sesame seeds

Servings: 4 portions

Total time: 20 min

Instructions:

1. In a medium-sized bowl, blend the chicken, chopped garlic, cooking sake, and cornstarch. Whisk well to make sure that all components are well combined. Allow the mixture to marinate for 15 minutes.
2. Prepare the stir-fry sauce by combining oyster sauce, lime juice, sweet chili sauce, Sriracha, and 1/4 cup of hot water in another bowl. Put aside or store the sauce in the fridge until ready to use.
3. Bring a big pot filled with 8 cups of water to a boil before cooking the noodles. Cook the dried noodles in the boiling water for about 8 minutes, uncovered.
4. When cooked, remove the noodles from the flame, drain them, and rinse with cold water to halt the cooking process. Set the noodles aside.

5. Heat a tablespoon of oil in a large 14-inch wok over high flame. Put the marinated chicken to the wok and stir-fry for 4-5 minutes, ensuring it is fully cooked and lightly browned. Transfer the cooked chicken to a plate.
6. Return the wok to the stove and set the heat to high. Put another tablespoon of oil to the wok. Toss in the broccolini and minced garlic, stirring quickly for a few seconds until the garlic becomes fragrant. Add the bell pepper and cabbage, continuing to stir-fry on high heat and tossing the vegetables constantly for approximately one minute until they are coated with a glossy glaze.
7. Introduce the cooked and drained noodles to the wok, followed by the stir-fry sauce. Using a large metal spatula or turner, continuously toss and stir-fry the noodles for 2-3 minutes, ensuring the sauce is evenly distributed and the noodles are well-coated.
8. Add the spring onions and the cooked chicken to the wok, tossing and stir-frying on high heat for an additional 2 minutes until everything is thoroughly heated. Taste the dish and correct the seasoning, if necessary, by adding flaky salt and black pepper. Mix all the ingredients together well.
9. Drizzle with sesame seeds for garnish and enjoy immediately.

Chicken with almonds

Ingredients:

- 1 tablespoon cornstarch
- 1 carrot
- 1 1/2 cups water
- 4.4 ounces mushrooms
- 2 tablespoons oil, extra
- 1 tablespoon soy sauce
- 1/2 of a 8-ounce can bamboo shoots
- 3 stalks celery
- 1 teaspoon grated fresh ginger
- 1 teaspoon salt
- 1 egg white
- shallots
- 1 chicken stock cube
- 4 chicken breast fillets
- 2.1 ounces blanched almonds
- 1 tablespoon dry sherry
- oil for deep-frying
- 1 tablespoon cornstarch
- 1 1/2 tablespoon dry sherry

Servings: 6 portions

Total time: 40 min

Instructions:

1. Slice the mushrooms into rough pieces. Cut the celery into diagonal slices. Divide the shallots into 1-inch segments. Thinly slice the bamboo shoots and cut them into strips measuring ½ inch. Peel and dice the carrot.
2. Remove any skin from the chicken breast fillets and cut the meat into 1-inch chunks. Combine the chicken with salt, cornstarch, lightly beaten egg white, and dry sherry. Ensure they are thoroughly mixed.
3. In a pan, heat some extra oil and add the almonds. Fry them until they get a golden-brown color. Remove from the pan and drain them on absorbent paper.
4. While the almonds are frying, prepare the sauce. Blend cornstarch with water, soy sauce, dry sherry, and crumbled chicken stock cube. Whisk the mixture over medium heat until the sauce boils and thickens.
5. Add the grated green ginger and diced carrots to the pan. Gently fry them for one minute before adding the remaining vegetables.

138

6. Sauté until the vegetables are soft but still retain some crispness, stirring occasionally. Incorporate the cooked chicken into the mixture and heat everything thoroughly. Pour in the sauce, making sure it is well mixed with the other ingredients.
7. Finally, stir in the fried almonds.

Traditional fried ice cream

Ingredients:

- 1 cup all-purpose flour
- 1 teaspoon baking soda
- Powdered sugar for dusting, optional
- Vegetable oil to deep fry should not have flavor
- Chocolate syrup and whipped cream for garnish if desired
- 1 teaspoon vanilla extract
- 1 egg
- 1 cup ice-cold water
- 2 cups ice cream (you can use any flavor)
- completely frozen ice cubes

Servings: 4 portions

Total time: 2h 20 min

Instructions:

1. Make ice cream scoops with a scoop for ice cream and set them on a baking sheet. Top with a transparent film and place in the freezer for 2 hours for the night to firm up.
2. Fill a large bowl with ice cubes.
3. Sift the flour together with the baking soda into a smaller bowl and put it inside the ice-filled bowl.
4. Lightly beat the egg in another bowl until it starts to froth.
5. Mix in the cooled water and vanilla extract with the beaten egg. Blend together the egg mixture and the flour mixture until just combined. Avoid excessive mixing.
6. Preheat the oil for frying to a depth of about 2 inches, maintaining a temperature between 350°F and no higher than 400°F.
7. Grab the ice cream balls out of the freezer. Get one ball and soak it into the tempura batter.
8. Carefully drop the coated ice cream ball into the hot oil and fry for approximately 30 seconds until the batter turns a pale brown color.
9. Serve immediately. If desired, top with chocolate syrup and whipped cream.

- *Please scan this QR code and enjoy all the instructions in the video!*

- *Here's the link, copy and paste it into your browser:*

https://me-qr.com/A8ucbu0S

Conclusion

And here we are at the end of this cookbook. I want to clarify and finalize a few but essential concepts that this book of mine wants to convey. This sushi recipe book is your gateway to not only mastering the art of sushi-making but also embracing a healthy and balanced lifestyle. Sushi, renowned for its exquisite flavors and artistic presentation, is not just a culinary delight, but also a nutritious and wholesome choice.

The Japanese have long been admired for their longevity, and their well-balanced diet plays a significant role in their extended lifespan. Sushi, with its emphasis on fresh seafood, nutrient-rich vegetables, and nourishing ingredients, embodies the essence of this healthy eating philosophy.

By following the recipes in this book, you're not only learning how to create delectable sushi rolls but also incorporating a wide range of essential nutrients into your diet. From omega-3 fatty acids found in fish to the vitamins and minerals abundant in vegetables, sushi offers a wealth of health benefits.

Moreover, the meticulous preparation and precise portion sizes of sushi encourage mindful eating, promoting a sense of satiety and portion control. This mindful approach to food can help maintain a healthy weight and a balanced lifestyle.

However, I want to assure you that sushi-making is a skill that can be learned and perfected with practice. Don't be discouraged by the intricacies—embrace them as opportunities for growth and creativity.

So, as you embark on your sushi-making journey, you're not just mastering a culinary skill, but also embracing a lifestyle that fosters longevity and well-being. Let this recipe book be your companion in creating nutritious, flavorful, and visually stunning sushi creations that will nourish both your body and soul.

With clear instructions, simplified techniques, and a focus on balanced ingredients, this book assures you that sushi-making is an accessible and enjoyable endeavour.

In conclusion, I would like to express my sincere gratitude to all of you for placing your trust in me. I would be glad to hear about your experiences in the kitchen with my recipe book.

I am deeply grateful to my father for instilling in me a love for poetry, history, and most importantly, the culinary arts. What started as a hobby has now become my profession.

Lastly, I want to extend my gratitude to my friends who, through their continuous requests for new recipes, inspired me to create a cookbook that could help everyone achieve outstanding sushi at home, just like in a restaurant.

Made in United States
North Haven, CT
18 November 2023

44198728R00080